Records from the Ancestral Mirror

Yongming Yanshou

Records from the Ancestral Mirror

宗鏡錄

Fascicles Two, Three and Four

Translated from the Original Chinese
by Randolph S. Whitfield

FSC
www.fsc.org
MIX
Papier aus ver-
antwortungsvollen
Quellen
Paper from
responsible sources
FSC® C105338

Fragrance
of the
Dharma
Hōkun Trust

The Hokun Trust is pleased to support this volume
of fascicles two, three and four
of
Yongming Yanshou's

Records from the Ancestral Mirror

Zongjing Lu 宗鏡錄

translated by

Randolph S. Whitfield.

Contents

Preface · 7
Acknowledgements · 9
A Note on Translation · 10
About the *Zongjing Lu* · *12*

Chan Master Yongming Yanshou's Message · 20
Fascicle Two · 23
Fascicle Three · 73
Fascicle Four · III

Appendix One · 153
Appendix Two · 162
Bibliography · 164
Index I · 168
General Index · 174

Preface

Many have discussed the *Zongjing lu* (hereafter ZJL), *Records from the Ancestral Mirror,* but none, except Albert Welter in his groundbreaking book *Yongming Yanshou's Conception of Chan* (hereafter YYCC),[1] have begun translating even one whole fascicle out of the hundred constituting this work – not surprising given the sheer volume and complex challenges this work poses. This small volume is a contribution to the work first set in motion by Welter – but without going into many of the subtleties of Yanshou's gnosis. The reader is directed to Welter's book for its wealth of information and insights, which also contains the first ever fully annotated translation into any language of the first fascicle.

The task I have set myself is more modest: to produce a more or less readable English rendition of fascicles two, three and four of this work. In the act of translating such a text, one has naturally to split hairs right down to their atoms, so that readers can profit from such dissections, always hidden in the background; but it needs to be born in mind that the original goal of such a work as Yanshou's (and there are many of them, in Chinese, Korean and Japanese) was to edify, educate, stimulate and ultimately to inspire some to take up the study and practice of the Buddha-dharma. Hopefully this still holds good today.

The current translation then, aspires to be readable, but it is not 'popular' – there is no paraphrasing and indeed, if a *bona fide* criticism could be levelled at it (leaving aside the howlers), it is perhaps that it is a too literal rendition.

Yanshou's lengthy quotations from the sources he cites in fascicles two, three and four are also an interesting entrée for those of us who have no easy access to his technical and protean vocabulary.

I have confined myself to translation and some meandering: interested readers should consult Albert Welter's works and bibliographies as a proper introduction to the background of Chan 'history'.

In the footnotes the provenance of a cited work on its first appearance is given, for the sake of affording a glimpse into Yanshou's mental world; after

---

[1] Welter, Albert. *Yongming Yanshou's Conception of Chan in the Zongjing Lu.* See also 'Beyond Lineage Orthodoxy: Yongming Yanshou's Model of Chan as Bodhisattva Cultivation' *Chung-Hwa Buddhist Journal* (2013, 26: 1–31) New Taipei: Chung-Hwa Institute of Buddhist Studies 1–31. ISSN: 1017–7132.

that, only the (usually) Taisho number is given. Page and section beginnings of the Taisho text are indicated by bold letters in square brackets within the translation.

Two appendices are included:
   i) a complete numerical list (79 in number) of the cited works in fasc. 2–4
   ii) the biographical entry for Yongming Yanshou (edited) from the *Jingde Chuandeng lu* (hereafter CDL)

I have not provided the Chinese for fascicles two, three and four – these are widely available on multiple websites.

Acknowledgements

In gratitude
to
The Hokun Trust
and to
Michelle Bromley
for supporting the publication of this volume.

A Note on Translation

A note on *xin* 心, usually translated as *heart* or *mind*.

'… if the etymology of the word 'translation' had suggested, say, the image of responding to an existing utterance instead of transference, the whole idea of a transfer postulate would probably never have arisen' Theo Hermans, *Translation in Systems:* p.52, cited in Maria Tymoczko, *Enlarging Translation, Empowering Translators,* p.6.

'… because in any literary work there will remain multiple interpretations resulting from the inherent openness of literary texts and language itself, the limit of convergence [for determinacy in translation] will generate a family of interpretations rather than a single "correct" reading to be embodied in the translation,' Maria Tymoczko, *Translation Postcolonial,* p.156.

It could be said that the whole of the *Zongjing Lu* is an exposition of the single Chinese character *xin* 心, omnipresent in this work; it occurs more than twelve *thousand* times. Indeed, *xin* is arguably the central character in all of Chinese Buddhism and one of the most frequently occurring characters in Chinese secular culture, ancient and modern.[2]

What is *xin* 心? It is usually translated into English as either *mind* or *heart*. But *xin* takes on many nuances of meaning and is therefore highly context sensitive. Feeling, thinking, gnosis, ineffable intent, unconditioned Being, the unborn; also a psycho-spiritual organ; epicentre of emptiness, a bridge between the phenomenal and noumenal world, confused *xin*, afflicted *xin* and so on. Edward Slingerland has translated *xin* as 'heart/mind' in his book on *wuwei*.[3] Taking one step further I began by translating it without the forward slash, as *heartmind,* but was by no means happy with this solution; it is just too heavy

---

[2] *Xin* is number 90 in the top 8943 of Chinese [single] characters, https://hanzicraft.com/lists/frequency, number 135 from the *Leiden Weibo Corpus* (LWC) of 1,371,991 words (including combinations). http://lwc.daanvanesch.nl/frequentwords.php

[3] Slingerland, E. *Effortless Action Wu-wei as Conceptual Metaphor.*

in many contexts. Furthermore, where would this mind / heart be located, in the *mind*? If the Chan / Buddhist *mind* is located in the brain, where presumably *mind,* its usual translation, is housed, then in which half of the brain? Heart in the right brain, mind in the left?

Synonyms of *xin* 心 as *consciousness* are *shi* 識 and *yi* 意, though *xin* has a more global meaning. In Abhidharma and Yogacara, *shi* 識 is the function of the six faculties perceiving the six objects, often synonymous with *xin* 心 and *yi* 意. In eight consciousness theory *yi* 意 is a term for the seventh (*manas* 末 那識), calculating consciousness, the sixth *manovijñāna* 意識 conceptualising consciousness, is usually expressed as *shi* 識.

Still, 'There are many ways of going forward, but only one way of standing still'.[4] I would have much preferred to keep the character *xin* untranslated throughout the text, but am aware that this might not speak to readers unfamiliar with its many nuances. An obvious translation for *xin* therefore, which I have adopted for this translation, is *consciousness,* which just about covers everything. Even today, scientists do not know what consciousness *is*, the Buddhists do also not know: nobody knows.[5]

Master Yongming Yanshou, author of the *Zongjing Lu,* clearly states that, 'The deluded consciousness (*xin*) is the shadowy form of the true consciousness above it'.[6] This shadow consciousness is afflicted by affective confusions – greed, anger and delusion; the higher consciousness is the same consciousness but liberated from these. Consciousness (*xin*) then, is not reducible to right brain intuition, left brain rationality, to heart or mind. 'Being so, this universal consciousness is not like that of worldlings, who absurdly regard it as capable of being deduced from conditions and grasp with certitude that it is [all] in the physical body.[7]

---

[4]   Franklin D. Roosevelt.

[5]   The intrinsic nature (自體) of true consciousness is not something to be explained in words. It is as deep as boundless space, 真心自體非言所詮湛如無際之虛空. T48.426b27.

[6]   妄心是真心上之影 Ibid:, 431b01.

[7]   Ibid.: 425b01.

About the *Zongjing Lu*

Today, as yesterday, Chinese religiosity is rich in its variety of received influences: from Buddhist India, from Sinitic Daoism, Confucianism and from an original, home-grown Buddhism, including Chan. In China this eclectic approach has ever been the norm:[8] rigidity in religious affiliations seems alien to Asian sensibilities.

The *Zongjing Lu* is not a typical [Song dynasty] 'Chan' text – it does not seek to delight the reader with an original brilliance expressing wisdom and insight. The work is studious, traditional Buddhist logic, conforming to a time-honoured Indo-Sinitic analysis of the human condition and its transcendence.

Yongming Yanshou (904–976 CE) refers to himself as a Chan Master. For more than a thousand years he has been a figure difficult to squeeze into a tiny box of preconceptions regarding what a 'Chan master' really is.[9] Most inconveniently, he was also the sixth *patriarch* of Pure Land practices,[10] so how could he be a *pure* Chan master?[11] This originally Indian Pure Land movement[12] was/is all-pervasive in Asian Mahayana traditions without being/possessing

---

[8] See Eric Zürcher's seminal article "Perspectives in the Study of Chinese Buddhism." 'It can be demonstrated that, as soon as we go below that top level, quite another picture emerges, in which Buddhism loses much of its sharp contour, as it is absorbed into the surrounding mass of Chinese indigenous religion.' *Journal of the Royal Asiatic Society* 1982 (2): 161–176.

[9] 'Perhaps neglect is the fate of a work that does not fit neatly into the traditionally demarcated categories of Chinese religion that dominate modern scholarship.' Robson, *Power of Place*, p. 96.

[10] For a discussion of Yanshou as a master (patriarch) of the Pure Land see Welter, *YYCC: 27ff.*

[11] 'Though Chan and Pure Land sectarians developed sophisticated, mutually differential hermeneutics that attempted to determine a hierarchy between effort and grace, it can be argued that most East Asian Buddhists continued to seek assurance from both.' Wendy Adamek, *The Mystique of Transmission*, p.108.

[12] 'The [*Pratyutpanna-buddha-sarpmukhavasthita-samadhi-Sūtra*] (abbrv.) *PraS* is well-known for containing the earliest dateable mention of the Buddha Amitābha/Amitayus; however, because of the later history of the text in China and Japan its Pure Land aspect has often been over-emphasised.' Paul Harrison. See note 16.

a definite 'doctrine'. *Our* Western Land (Paradise Lost) is rather squeamish about chanting or visualisation practices, as if the [Christian] devil himself were being invoked: not very respectable. Yet given an all-embracing Mahayana Buddhism in south-east China of the 10th century, mirrored in the ZJL, a strong theophanic element in common practices of worship surrounding Yanshou and acolytes would seem to have been a likely part of daily life. Furthermore, the history of manifesting an apparition of a Buddhist *ipseity* through the contemplation/incantation of a *name*,[13] in this case Amitābha, so that the worshipper might see Him 'as clearly as seeing the stars in the night sky,'[14] has a long and venerable history in Chinese religion (and is also a common element in other world religions).[15] For, says Yanshou, quoting a famous sutra, Buddha Amitābha, the Western Paradise, is right here and now.[16] Nevertheless, Yanshou declares that calling upon Buddha Amitābha in the hope of gaining a good rebirth in his Western Paradise (*nianfo*) [17] is for persons who have no faith in their own consciousness being Buddha,[18] where *nianfo* is the entrance into the sanctuary of enlightenment.'[19]

---

[13] '*Subhuti*: What *dharanis* has he (the Bodhisattva) acquired so that he no longer forgets the Sutras taught by the Tathāgata? *The Lord*: The *dharani* which causes inexhaustibility, the Seal of the Ocean, and the Lotus Array.' Conze, *The Large Sutra,* p. 403.

[14] Zhiyi's phrase, T1911.46.0012a24 (see note 24). 'In Zhiyi's system …contemplative and devotional practices are subordinated to their own interdependence.' Adamek, *Mystique,* p.113.

[15] For a recent attempt to establish the Pure Land of *Maitreya* here on earth (ultimately unsuccessful after 1949), see the work of the modern Buddhist reformer Taixu 太虛 (1890–1947) in Pitman, *Towards a Modern Chinese Buddhism. Taixu's Reforms.* In the Christian *Spiritual Exercises* by Ignatius Loyola (1491–1556), for the second week of the retreat, one is to exercise *all* five imaginative senses (not just visualisation) on scenes from the Gospels in order to experience them *directly.* For an interesting account of early visualisation practices centred around Amitābha on Mount Lu see Zürcher, BCC: 220*ff*; ibid.: 194 for Daoan's *Maitreya* visualisations (T2059.50.353b28).

[16] T48.0559b21 西方阿彌陀佛今現在. For the background to T418 see Harrison, Paul. *The Samādhi of Direct Encounter with the Buddhas of the Present:* Appendix A.

[17] See Jones, *Chinese Pure Land Buddhism,* p.13 for a quotation from Yanshou (T.2016.48:506a10–a14) on this term (in fasc. 17 not 4) where Yanshou provides a rationale for this practice.

[18] 只為不信自心是佛 T48.0506a12.

[19] 一念知一切法是道場 皆是念佛法門也 'One thought-moment knows that every dharma (phenomenon) is the site of enlightenment – all [things] are the entrance to

If the *Pure Land* is a double projection from the believer's own *ālayavijñāna*,[20] is this one of the functions of 'Only Consciousness' (唯識), the constant refrain of the ZJL?[21] If you *believe* in Amitābha, he stands before you. Human feelings going out towards the Buddhas and their response to a consciousness of faith (*ganying* 感應) are heard, for 'Humans and the Buddhist pantheon and cosmos are bound tightly together via the mechanism of stimulus-response …the Buddhist unseen world is exquisitely responsive: it is not aloof and indifferent …nor is it capricious in its responses …'[22] Yanshou too, in the second fascicle, says that 'Human feelings and the response [of the Buddhas] is not unreal.' (非虛) (426c16)

Pure Land and Chan: in the *Jingde Chuandeng Lu* (CDL), Emperor Xuanzong (r. 847–859 CE) questions Chan master Hongbian of Da Jiangfu Temple in Jingzhou (Shanxi, Xi'an),

> 'What of the people of today who call upon Buddha?' Hongbian replied, '…
> for those of middling capacities, because they couldn't awaken suddenly,
> the Buddha therefore opened the temporarily expedient gate of the sixteen
> entrances to meditation and of invoking Buddha to be born in the Pure
> Land …'[23]

And Zongmi, in his *Chan Prolegomenon*, quoted in the CDL, says,

> Coming to recollection of the Buddha by seeking birth in the Pure Land,
> they must also cultivate the sixteen moments of seeing, as well as the sa-

recollecting the Dharma of the Buddhas.' Zhiyi, 四念處, Four Bases of Mindfulness. T1918.46.0574c02 / T2016.48. 0896c29.

20   There is a self-empowered pure *xin* and a pure *xin* of grace ('other power') 有自力淨 心 他力淨心 T48.0534b17.

21   Yanshou cites the [大乘]密嚴經 *Dasheng miyan jing, Ghana-vyūha* 'Great Vehicle Sutra of [the Pure Land], Densely Adorned' T681 / 682 frequently in the ZJL: here in fasc. 5, 如來清淨藏 世間阿賴耶 T48.0441a22; also in the second fasc., likening its explicit teachings with the *Laṅkāvatāra Sūtra* (note 178 below).

22   Robert Ford Campany, *Signs from the Unseen Realm*, p.49.

23   T2076.51.0269b21, in Randolph S. Whitfield, (trans.). *Records of the Transmission of the Lamp*, (hereafter RTL). **9.185**.

madhi of recollecting Buddha and [enter] the samadhi of seeing all the Buddhas of the ten directions [*as clearly as the stars at night*].[24]

What Chan practice and Pure Land chanting and visualisations obviously have in common is *faith*: these meditation practices take long years to cultivate, impossible without intense effort and whole-hearted *devotion*.[25] The isolated ego cannot sustain such intensity; disappointments and failure come quickly: faith is needed in *some form*. The strangeness of such meditation states centred around visualisations – and the attempt to study them second-hand – brings home how old masters of meditation such as Zhiyi and Yanshou (not to mention Daoists and Tibetans) were able to describe these states authoritatively, veritable *tours de force* of consciousness and *memory*, the direct personal experience, verified by the commensurate insight into our human potential.

Consciousness's power to visualise has been lauded in other civilised cultures;[26] it certainly exists, be it as a more or less protean/slippery non-entity, ungraspable physically or non-physically. According to Yanshou,

> The true consciousness (*xin*) – a ring of iron would not be able to conceal its radiance, for it pervades the three thousand great chiliocosms and the all-pervasive void. (T48.0432a19)

This is not mere hyperbole. Again, this off-world consciousness; experienced Buddhist meditation masters such as Zhiyi, Yanshou and many others, might

[24] Seeing '… *as clearly as the stars at night*' is actually Zhiyi's explication of 般舟三昧 *Pratyutpanna Samādhi,* 能於定中見十方現在佛在其前立如明眼人清夜觀星 (T1911.46.0012a24) but does not appear in the CDL, nor in Zongmi's *Chan Prolegomenon.* (*Pratyutpanna Samādhi,* MMW: 677c, 'existing in the present moment; regenerated.'). See the translation of the *Prolegomenon* by Broughton, *Zongmi on Chan,* p.103 and note 6, p, 244, where 般舟三昧 *Pratyutpanna Samādhi* is translated as 'engendered concentration'.

[25] 'Whole-hearted reverence is the first gate to the various meritorious powers,' 一心敬慎是諸功德初門 T48.632a19 quoting *Di Zhidu Lun,* T1509.25.129b26.

[26] 'The human Imagination is enveloped in the unconditioned Imagination, which is the universe as Divine Epiphany, for this envelopment is our guarantee that the intentions arising from the creative power of the heart as an independent being *sui generis,* are not vain fictions.' Henry Corbin, *Creative Imagination in the Ṣūfism of Ibn ʿArabi,* p.263. Ibn Arabi (1165–1240).

have achieved something quite notable: through years of both practical experience in meditation and of harvesting the insights of this experience (one half is not possible without the other), they managed to synchronise their two brain-halves to reveal a higher-consciousness above the deluded one,[27] responsible for producing incomprehensibly vast, profound and erudite literatures. Why otherwise would Yanshou say that 'One should stimulate consciousness as if it were a *bridge* in order to liberate oneself from forgetfulness and weariness,'[28] a direct quote from the *Huayan Jing.* [29] The key here is *the bridge,* the liminal nature of consciousness (橋梁心), not without its danger.[30] Pure Land practice originally concerned the art of dying, the importance of the last thought moment at death to ensure a propitious rebirth in the Western Paradise. One of Yanshou's *myriad good deeds*[31] might have been to stimulate this process to see/feel Amitābha *in this very life,* before physical death. Chan [meditation] and *Pure Land* practices seem to partner well in this undertaking, for 'the contemplation of emptiness is not hindered by the constant practice of recitation.'[32] It should also be born in mind that talk of students' middling or lesser capacities was not pejorative or discriminative: skilful means were acts of *compassion.* This all-embracing consciousness then is clearly a chip from the 'uncarved block', its true affinity. [33] Earthbound, with feet of clay, left and right brains work ever so slightly out of sync, a disconnect discernible even *in the written word.* Therefore, not to take the multiple contexts of consciousness into account – a *Chan/Pure Land* streaming out of and back into our consciousnesses, only consigns us to a learning place we never fully inhabit. Some 'ancients', released from their root afflictions, no longer sang in their chains like the sea – they *became* the sea.[34]

Yanshou's *magnum opus* is the *Zongjing Lu* 宗鏡錄, translated here as *Records*

---

[27] T48.0431b01, 妄心是眞心上之影像. An insight with a venerable pedigree – Plotinus, Ibn ʻArabī *et al.*

[28] 應發如橋梁心濟渡忘疲故 ibid.: 661a08.

[29] T0279.10.0421c18.

[30] 從獨木橋上過亦不教伊倒地 T48.945c10.

[31] Welter, *Myriad Good Deeds.*

[32] Fazang talking, T1878.45.0652a01/T48.421c16.

[33] *Laozi,* ch. 28.

[34] Dylan Thomas, *Fern Hill,* 'Time held me green and dying/Though I sang in my chains like the sea.'

from the Ancestral Mirror. The character *zong* 宗,[35] like consciousness (*xin*), takes on multiple nuances.[36] The jury might be out forever on what Yanshou's understanding of *zong* is in relation to Chan. Further, the combination of two key but unrelated Chinese Buddhist characters, *zong* (宗) and mirror (鏡) is peculiar to Yanshou, who uses the combination (宗鏡) more than five hundred times in the total ZJL, defining his meaning as the facilitator of a two-way traffic, 'attracting Buddha-wisdom teachings into the ancestral-mirror (from the realm of birthlessness) to reveal it outwardly as the path of Buddhist practice,'[37] a skilful means provided for sentient beings' return to the birthless. Might it be then, that Yanshou's use of *zong* in the title of his work also embraces 'ancestors' as guardians reflecting the *source* of [Buddhist] truth, for he calls upon them, as he says himself (fasc.94), three hundred times in the ZJL; and quotes from them, sometimes extensively, some seven thousand times.

Yet a mirror cannot reveal things 'as they really are'. The English saying 'as above, so below' hints at the problem of mirrors: their images are a reversal of the original, of 'reality', or, they reveal the shadow side of the real. The image in the mirror then could be taken as false, reversed, counterfeit, lacking essence, illusory. 'Reality' itself would seem to be unapproachable, unknowable, so 'nothing is real'; hence the 'Chan' encouragement to have faith but not to believe: to taste for oneself, to get behind the image, the appearance, to the non-existent real, which is but a call to action.

The mirror then might be a passageway into *another* reality, a gateway into the realm of inversion. Outside becomes inside, inside, outside; reality, appearance, appearance, reality. The less covered in dust the mirror is, the more accurate the reflection: yet the more accurate the reflection, the greater the horror of imperfection seeing itself, a trauma, a catharsis, from which only practitioners might ever fully recover. The mirror can kill both ways, either by strengthening vanity, in which case it effectively kills spiritual life, or by destroying vanity,

---

[35] Ancestral temple, ancestral, lineage (which performs ancestor worship), royal clan; to venerate, honour. *ABC Etymological Dictionary of Old Chinese*, Axel Schuessler.

[36] YYCC: 48*ff.* Welter translates *zong* as 'source' and glosses it as 'implicit truth.'(YYCC: 223.) Fazang has an extensive treatment of *zong* in his commentary on the *Laṅkâvatāra Sutra*, T1790.39.42b18*ff.*

[37] T48.424b24 宗鏡中始終引佛智慧之教光 顯佛所行之道跡.

in which case it kills me, the 'I' as I know myself; then it is possible to pass through, but only by shattering it.[38]

The images in Yanshou's mirror are many, his Chan atypical. He is reported to have recited the *Lotus Sutra* thirteen thousand times during his life: image-making.[39] Some of his contemporaries seem more in the mainstream of what came to be regarded as 'Chan'.[40] There was, for example, Chan master Fadeng Taiqin (910?-974), an almost exact contemporary of Yanshou, also active in the south-east. Taiqin was a disciple of Fayan Wenyi (885–958/9), the master of Yanshou's master Tiantai Deshao (891–972). Yet Yanshou and Taiqin, though from the same spiritual stable, seem poles apart: Taiqin is original, Yanshou traditional; Taiqin is piquant, Yanshou studious. Taiqin has a marked presence in the *Jingde Chuandeng Lu,* with more than two entries of his own and many interlinear comments on others, where he is often paired with Fayan Wenyi. One of Taiqin's Dharma-heirs, Yunju Daoqi (929–997) also appears in the CDL; his heirs numbered fifty-four persons. Yet Yanshou and Taiqin also share the same Chan talk at times: for example, the *'ancient* mirror' (古鏡) is a favourite metaphor in the Chan *yulu* (recorded sayings) genre. Yanshou: 'Find your original face in front of the ancient mirror.' Taiqin: 'Just trust in being able to see your face [in the ancient mirror].[41]

---

[38] 'If there is the slightest blemish (on the ancient mirror) there is sickness / You would be better advised to smash it / Mirror gone, blemish vanished, it will just shine'. (Taiqin, *Song of the Ancestral Mirror*).

[39] Not to be taken literally. There is the practice of *zhuandu* 轉讀 (Jap. *tendoku*) – quick sutra recitation. 'Cursory reading: lit. 'revolving reading.' … specifically refers to turning the pages of the text and briefly chanting the title, along with lines from the beginning, middle, and ending portions. Especially noted as a practice for the reading of such large scriptures as the *Prajñāpāramitā-Sūtra*. The main point of this practice is to make merit 功德 that is then dedicated 廻向 in support of some prayer. Also written 轉經 and 略讀. Distinguished from 'real reading' 眞讀.' DDB: Charles Muller, Griffith Foulk. On the physical text of sutras as cult objects see Daniel B. Stevenson, 'Buddhist Practice and the *Lotus Sutra* in China' in *Readings of the Lotus Sutra*, p.132–150.

[40] Yunmen Wenyan 雲門文偃 (864–949) and his Dharma heir Xianglin Chengyuan 香林澄遠 (908–987); Fengxue Yanzhao 風穴延沼 (896–973); Shoushan Shengnian 首山省念 (926–993) – all were contemporaries active in different areas north and south of the river.

[41] The whole of the Chan Dharma is contained in these lines. Fadeng Taiqin's 法燈禪師泰欽 entry in CDL, T2076.414c04; RTL: 25.883; See his three poems in the CDL *Song of the Ancient Mirror* 古鏡歌三首, T2076.463a05; RTL: 30.18. 但任作見面,

The *Zongjing Lu* does include accounts of Chan masters (principally in fasc. 96 & 97); the *Jingde Chuandeng Lu*, a compendium of Chan wisdom and insight, published fifty years later in 1011 CE, did become the *locus classicus* of the Chan Dharma. Both express a contemporary setting, a *differentiation* of various inchoate Chan establishments embedded in an environment of a fluid Buddhism[42] prevalent in south-east China at the beginning of the Song dynasty (960–1279 CE).

Even though China was a highly conservative society, one still wonders at the depth, after eight or nine centuries of its reception of Buddhism, to which they were still steeped in the Indian traditions of the Mahayana (as reflected in the ZJL). In any case, there was no *Chinese* scholastic Buddhism that was not wholly based on Indian models. Contrast this with the almost dramatic originality, the freshness of the appearance of a developing Chan *culture* epitomised in its foundational text, the *Jingde Chuandeng Lu* (CDL), seeming to jettison a thousand years of the most intense Chinese engagement with Indian Buddhism. The contrast between the two works, the *Zongjing Lu* and the *Jingde Chuandeng Lu,* could hardly seem greater; yet, these two mighty literary pillars, the one looking back a thousand years to a hallowed past, the other forward a thousand years into the future, between them formed the gateway through which countless generations of wayfarers (and *literati*) entered[43] and still enter, seeking a pointer to the way of release..

Nothing then, can take away the significance of the *Zongjing Lu*. To produce a complete translation and commentary of this work would make known to a wider world the richness of this all-encompassing Buddhism prevalent in 10th century south-east China, skilfully recorded by Chan master Yongming Yanshou.

T2076.51.0463a18. Yanshou: 得本頭於古鏡之前, T2016.416c06 (see also YYCC: 325, n. 50.). Yunju Daoqi 雲居道齊, T2076.428c03, RTL: 26.964, his heirs are listed in 續傳燈錄 T2077.51.0528c19.

[42] John R. McRae, '… lineage assertions that can be shown to be historically accurate are also inevitably inconsequential as statements of religious identity.' *Seeing Through Zen,* p. xix.

[43] For the Ming dynasty (1368–1644 CE) reinvention of Chan Buddhism see Jiang Wu, *Enlightenment in Dispute.* During the Qing dynasty (1644–1911 CE) the *Yongzheng* Emperor (雍正: r. 1723–1735 CE) compiled *The Imperial Record of the Main Principles of the Zongjing,* (L164.1668), printed by the Imperial Household in the twelfth year of Yongzheng's reign (1734). See Hummel, *Eminent Chinese,* vol.2, p. 915; esp. 918 on the Emperor's Chan Buddhist leanings.

Chan Master Yongming Yanshou's Message

Nothing is real
And nothing to get hung about[44]

In this twenty-first century 'Era of Crisis' Yongming Yanshou's message, were it divested of its Buddhist vocabulary, might be even more relevant, more urgent, than it was in his local area of south-east China in the tenth century. This 'Era of Crisis' now embraces our entire home-world: the earth, all plants, all animals, all humans.

Yanshou's message is simple but radical. Not content with expressing it in his own words, he backs them up by calling upon the ancestors of all schools of Buddhism. But it is not a new message; all the wise ones from antiquity have re-iterated it tirelessly.

The beauty of Yanshou's currency is that it is a single coin with, of course, two sides. The bare essence of the message is stamped on both sides with a single Chinese character –*xin* (心) *consciousness*, the only thing left to 'believe' in nowadays, since we are clearly all participants, along with the earth, plants and animals, in this mysterious phenomenon. One side of Yanshou's coin retains its pristine original shine, the other side is discoloured by various causes and conditions, yet it is the same coin. This consciousness in our world and beyond is the source of all doings and non-doings, from the very negative to the very positive and everything in between – all is underpinned by it.

Now it is easy enough to write about consciousness, easy enough to understand it intellectually in accord with one's particular biases, easy enough to preach on consciousness; but to be called to another level of it augurs irreversible changes in the individual and in the collective, involving an often initially uncomfortable adjustment to an ageless new (old) open road. The ancestors, the tiniest minority accessible through their literary records, the inconceivably huge majority still locked up in our own genetic codes, know well that it is not easy to come to another level of awakening to life's plenitude without the experience of suffering. Out of compassion and by skilful means the literate minority bestirred themselves to write about something which in print is just so much

---

[44] Lennon/McCartney, *Strawberry Fields Forever*, 1967.

waste paper. Yet were it not for those such as Yanshou, this message of 'only heart' (唯心 synonym for consciousness) might have been lost. But even given such an inconceivable occurrence, consciousness would remain unmoved, for it endures as long as Life itself endures.

All this waste paper then is for the sake of offering us, who cannot *believe* in anything anymore – huddled under the withering tree of 'knowledge'– one possible access of many into the precincts of what Buddhists call the realm of 'awakening'. This awakening, this realisation, is no fiction.

For the characteristics prevalent in all structures on our world is a web complex enough to defy a definitive description – let alone understanding – so that all that can ever be said is actually an imposition, a re-structuring, without intrinsic reality. It is like looking at the millions of stars in the night sky, seeing patterns in them and giving these patterns terrestrial names (such as Amitābha Buddha). Buddhism is a 'descriptive system' of practice developed for the purpose of breaking free from it. The same holds with the Chan game plan; its *description* is a map drawn in one particular mode using a certain projection system that has no intrinsic reality. What is this Chan game? Liken it to a spider in the middle of its web, weaving according to its nature yet influenced by its dependence on circumstances.[45]

Temporality is one hallmark of our world and of the lives of its members, where reality is governed by particular, though unknown, precedent circumstances producing a particular state at a particular time – this is its *quiddity*. Cause is simply a totality of states produced from one condition and a totality of conditions producing one state. This means that unresolved energetic interpenetrations – the life-blood of this world – lawfully separate from their combined causes by collision with another set of related combined causes, creating an interruption in both 'streams' that rends their flow asunder for a moment. In the breach, the birth of new possibilities is conceived – but only for an instant. The problem is that the formative forces of living bodies are born fully operational and programmed to deal with such intrusive breaks cutting across their flow – a process rightly called adaptability. By virtue of being so flexible, the repair of the breach before the fruition of new possibilities has had a chance to see the light of day is quick and automatic, whilst the impact is slow to sink in on

---

[45] Bees make honey, spiders weave webs, all inconceivable, all equipped with the heart's liberative function. 黃蜂作蜜 蜘蛛作網 皆不可思議 皆有心數法之解脫也 (fasc. 30) T48.592b10.

an awareness that is curiously habituated to ignoring such breaks in its fear to play safe. Again, breaks in the flow are possibilities for the emergence of latent seeds waiting to sprout, conferring the opportunity to assume more responsibility in steering the course of the ongoing life stream into new directions. When such a gap in the stream is noticed (these processes usually take place in the dark) and skilfully taken advantage of – as a result of familiarity in playing with Buddhist practice procedures – then a rejuvenation of natural vitality is conferred which is the opposite of a decline; it is a natural regeneration because it is a small return to the birthless.

The astonishing discovery made by Chan Buddhists who venture into this practice is that the nirvanic 'other world' is in fact a fresh re-entry into our very own everyday life but seen now in a pristine light never even conceived possible before. It is the view of our world seen from the phenomenal *and* from the Universal All – a matched pair yet without any separation; Only Consciousness.

Records from the Ancestral Mirror
by
Chan Master Yongming Yanshou

Fascicle Two

Now, the realm of all the Buddhas is quiescent, the world of living beings empty. What then are the causes and conditions giving rise to the marks of the Buddhas' teachings? (教迹)

Answer: Although in the fundamental reality (一實諦中) there is no arising or cessation, within the precinct of expedient means, causes and conditions are of great [import], hence a gatha in the *Fahua Jing* (Lotus Sutra) says,

> All dharmas forever lack inherent existence (常無性)
> The Buddha-seed arises from conditions[46]

Since all things forever lack inherent existence, when there is no lack of inherent existence, such dharmas do accord with conditions;[47] their empty nature is not lost in according with conditions. Moreover, the arising of the teachings depends on it. There is no limit to causes and conditions, as the ancient worthies have succinctly indicated. [Nevertheless], there are these ten kinds [of causes and conditions]: the first is due to the real nature of Dharma (or: to things as they really are 法爾); the second is due to the power of vows; the third, to the innate response [of Buddhas to living beings, of living beings to the Buddhas]; the fourth is due to the root/source; the fifth is due to the manifestation

---

[46] 妙法蓮華經玄義 *Miaofa lianhua jing xuanyi*, 'The Profound Meaning of the Sutra on the Lotus of the Marvellous Dharma', Zhiyi's commentary on the Lotus Sutra. T1716.33.0789c06.

[47] Dependent arising.

of innate virtue (顯德); the sixth, to the appearance of the ranks [of awakening]; the seventh, to awaken others; the eighth is due to it being seen and heard; the ninth to putting it into practice and the tenth is due to attaining fruition.

Now the great bodhisattvas have left us such collections as *Discourse on Only [Projections of] Consciousness*,[48] of which the main tenets are of two kinds: the first is to awaken to the correct transmission of the teachings concerning all dharmas and to resolve (destroy) the pernicious attachment to the two emptinesses;[49] the second is to break the afflictions that are a hindrance to knowing and realise the gate to the liberation of bodhi. This is the way to testify for oneself to the true ground of the Dharma as innate awakening [421c] – it is not in words and phrases that the meaning is elaborated but they are for students of a later generation who long for the Way.

The compilations are expedient means which also have a twofold intention by informing about the basic purpose. One is to summarise the essential points for those who like to have an outline in order to understand the essential pointers, whilst avoiding the complexities of looking through a complicated text. The second is for people to grasp the general purport but who are not clear about the distinct principle.[50]

To subtly expound on the noumenon and phenomena, fully penetrated, is to cut off the two roots of birth and death. Treading the single taste of the way of awakening and looking up to the great purport of the sutras means to understand directly one's own consciousness (自心). Following the subtle words of the sages, the treasure house of awakening suddenly opens. Attachments to common views removed, the perverse grasping to sentiments broken, there is deep faith in the impartial Buddhist teachings (正宗). The realisation is that the moon is not in the finger pointing to it but in returning the light to reflect within, which engenders an insight into the [true] nature, which can only testify to true principle, rather than following a text. This is the original intent.

48　唯識論 *Wéishì lun*, Prajñāruci's 般若流支 translation (6th century) of Vasubandhu's *Viṃśatikā-vijñapti-mātratā-siddhi* (*Viṃśatikākārikā*). T 1588.31 (also T1589; 1590).

49　破二空之邪執. Also 二無我 two forms of selflessness. The two categories of *anātman*: the lack of such a thing as substantial personhood 人無我 and the lack of a substantial essence in phenomena 法無我.

50　理 *li* – 'Original truth or universal principle. [...] this term was invested with a special meaning by the *Huayan* school, as the underlying 'noumenon' or principle of emptiness contained in and which contains all individual phenomena.' Charles Muller.

Do not perversely give rise to discursive knowledge, drowning in a river of opinions. In the contemplation of the inapprehensible, one harbours the intention to hasten there, approaching true emptiness as the main principle. Arousing the consciousness of taking up and letting go, pursuing one's own broadening of consciousness (胸襟), students leave doubts and mistakes behind. It is necessary to gain insight into the [true] nature for oneself, only then will this Buddhist [Chan] source (宗) be awoken to.

421c12

Question: Since there is a worry about grasping at the finger pointing and running after texts then, again, why be concerned about collecting teachings?

421c13

Answer: It is because of turning the back on oneself and mingling with the worldly dust. There is a fear of understanding the whole text, that the teachings will be an obstruction and bring about a blockage of deluded feelings; that is the reason for talk like this. Yet if the comments are followed up and the pointers understood, then the teachings will illumine consciousness, so what would there be to gather up and let go of? Therefore Master Fazang said,

> Certainly there are sentient beings searching the teachings in order to come to the real, without impediments to understanding principle; consistently contemplating principle they are not at all hindered by holding on to the teachings. The contemplation of emptiness is not hindered by the constant practice of recitation,[51] so all the true teachings can blend together, combining into a single contemplation; this is therefore the ultimate transmission – the oneness of teachings and contemplation. Comments and pointers are of the same source.[52]

421c19

Question: All the major sutras and commentaries have come from so many fragments, with an ordering principle into divisions and prefaces. The mean-

---

[51] Fazang's experience resonating with Yanshou's.

[52] 華嚴發菩提心章 *Huayan fa puti xin zhang,* 'Essay on the Huayan [School's] Arousal of Heart's Intention to Achieve Awakening' by Fazang 法藏 (643–712 CE), third patriarch of the school. T1878.45.0652a01.

ings of the sentences are clarified, but why bring together the records of a big text artificially and complete it with a summary?

421c21

Answer: It is only because the ocean of the teachings is so vast and deep that no one is able to come to its end or know its limits. Its meaning is as high and broad as heaven; looking up to it there is no arriving at its boundary. However, nowadays we use a pipe to peep into the heavens, take a snail's shell to scoop up the ocean, as if trying to scoop up a trickle of a cold blue stream with both hands or like gathering up a speck of dust from Mt. Taihua.[53] Originally, due to the meaning being broad and difficult to encompass, sentiments remained apathetic; also, because of not relying on the true principle of the One-vehicle (Mahayana), the significance of causal conditions is just seized on, not comprehended. Rarely coming to the gate of the relative and absolute, there is no knowledge of the place of arising and cessation, hence complexities are eliminated, differences simplified, the mysterious picked out and a search made of profundities.

Although the text is insufficient, yet the overall meaning is complete; [although] the conditions are not perfect, yet the correct principle is revealed. Searching the indications in the One-vehicle exhaustively, the choice is to open up the source to the ten thousand dharmas, the mysterious pivot being *prajñā* [wisdom], creating the essential path to awakening: then, with this preparation, [the path] will be easy of accomplishment. Hastening to reach the great vehicle of the Mahayana, the entry into realisation will be without doubts, avoiding circuitous and irrelevant paths. [**422a**] Therefore Aśvagoṣa Bodhisattva composed the treatise on *The Awakening of Faith in the Mahayana,* saying,

> Perhaps there are those without the power of wisdom (智), but due to the extensive discussions of others arrive at an understanding of the meaning; there again, there might be those, having no power of wisdom, who fear extensive explanations. Happy to hear abridged discussions that capture the broad meaning, they can then engage in correct practice. Now, for the sake of those latter people, I will briefly gather together the Tathāgata's supreme, profound and limitless meanings, to compose this treatise. [54]

---

[53] A mountain in Shaanxi.

[54] 大乘起信論 *Dasheng Qiconsciousness Lun,* 'The Awakening of Faith in the Mahayana'

In the *Yogâcārabhūmi-śāstra* it says,

> There are two reasons for writing this treatise: the first is because the Tathāgata's unsurpassed teachings of the Dharma have endured in the world; the second is for the sake of benefiting the welfare of all sentient beings equally. Again, it is because the sweet dew of the Tathāgata's sagely teachings has already sunk into obscurity, so to remember, gather and reveal those not yet sunk into obscurity. Propitious times determine questions and answers so again, they are gathered for the benefit of those diligently practising who delight in the abbreviated teachings and to gather together the broad essentials of the meanings of the Dharma from many sutras and clarify them succinctly.[55]

This constitutes the present record, though it lacks the merit of a broad scope in its composition, and even if there is no great overriding merit in its establishment, the time for a complete narration is extremely limited. It is also known that the record will be copied in its entirety, [though] the literary power is not even.

What is hoped for is that the most important points are selected for comment and further, that they will clarify the aim of the Buddhist source, like differentiating jade from stone or panning gold from sand. Selected from the many medicines is only the wonderful antidote[56] to the disease, which is directed towards the inner treasure of beings, solely to locate the wish-fulfilling jewel, for it alone will be upheld, putting all others into the shade. By taking the root and subsuming the branches, not a single word will be left unsaid. To put it differently, there is no alternative route, so it is also hoped that worthies of a later generation will not come down with ridicule and reprimands. What is wished for is to cut off doubt in order to give rise to faith, simply by means of seeing the

attributed to Aśvaghoṣa 馬鳴, translation attributed to Śikṣānanda 實叉難陀 (early 8th century).T1667.32.0584b18.

[55] 瑜伽師地論釋 *Yuqieshidilun shi, Yogâcārabhūmi-śāstra*, 'Treatise and Elucidation of the Stages of Yoga Practice' by Jinaputra 最勝子, translation by Xuanzang 玄奘 in 650. T1580.30.0883a17.

[56] *A-tuo* 阿陀 *agada* is one of the eight branches into which Ayurvedic medicine is traditionally divided. Literally, *gada* means a disease and a*gada* means any agent that makes the body free from disease.

Way as something harboured in the breast. It is not to chase after empty names as a means of inviting worldly praise.

The desire is to reach an opening for the future; within the endlessly pervasive Dharma realm, to pass through aeons and births beyond [measure] and always promote this Way. Those with heart (consciousness) can all enter this Buddhist source. To abandon attachments and extirpate doubts is to see and hear the benefits obtained. To inherit the power of the Three Treasures,[57] empower and maintain them. Vow to requite the compassion of the Buddhas, to generously aid sentient beings in order that emptiness may be reached. May these wishes not change, though the realm of Dharma be exhausted; may this text not fall into ruin.

422a22

Question: To awaken to the meaning of the great vehicle of the Mahayana, expanded, abbreviated or all-inclusive, understanding one meaning confers the insight of perfect penetration; hearing a single gatha has the ability of turning one into a Buddha. Why presume to be able to relate it completely or bother with an elucidation?

422a24

Answer: to a person of most excellent root faculties, one hearing is a thousand awakenings. The [true] nature and its [phenomenal] characteristics are complimentarily articulated, principle and phenomena perfectly proportioned. Concerning disciples of middling or lesser [root faculties] it is necessary to provisionally rely on opening an elucidation to the adornments of the Way. The praise and enhancement of the teachings (門), the measure of its merits, cannot but be served by metaphor. Therefore a gatha in the *Huafa Jing* says,

> The example is with the Udumbara flower[58]
> Each and every one is a delight
> Rare to appear amongst devas and humans
> Only emerging once in a long while
> Hearing the Dharma, joyful in praise
> Even emitting a single word

---

57 The Buddha, the Dharma and the Sangha.
58 *Ficus glomerate*; it is said to flower once every three thousand years.

Is already an offering proffered
To all the Buddhas of the three worlds
This is an exceedingly rare person
Surpassing the Udumbara flower[59]

A gatha in a commentary on the *Mahāprajñāparamitā-Sūtra* says, **[422b]**

Prajñā is indestructible
Being beyond all words
It inclines to no support
Who could praise its virtuous power?

Although it is impossible to praise *prajñā*
I now come to praise it
Although the stage of death is not yet escaped
Still, liberation has already been obtained[60]

An ancient worthy has also said,

If a bodhisattva composes a treatise it is referred to as a classic adornment, like a lotus flower yet to open; although seeing it evokes pleasure, it is not as good as the sweet perfume of one already opened; it is like gold yet to be put to use – seeing it evokes pleasure but it is not as good as fashioning it into an ornament.[61]

---

[59] 妙法蓮華經 *Miaofa lianhua jing, Saddharmapuṇḍarīka-Sūtra,* 'Sutra of the Lotus of the Wonderful Dharma' translated by Kumārajīva in 406 CE. T0262.09.0010a28.

[60] 大智度論 *Da Zhidu Lun, Mahāprajñāpāramitā-śāstra,* 'Commentary on the Mahaprajnaparamita-sutra' attributed to Nāgârjuna, translated by Kumārajīva. T1509.25.0190c27. For a discussion of the 'symbiotic' relationship between the sutra and the shastras, see Stefano Zacchetti, *The Da zhidu lun* 大智度論 *(*Mahāprajñāpāramitopadeśa) and the History of the Larger Prajñāpāramitā.* Also Lewis R. Lancaster, *An Analysis of the Aṣṭasāhasrikā-prajñāpāramitā-Sūtra from the Chinese Translations.* The *Da Zhidu Lun* was translated by Etienne Lamotte, *Traité de la Grande Vertu de Sagesse.*

[61] 成唯識論述記 *Cheng weishilun shuji,* 'A commentary on the *Cheng weishi lun*' 成唯識論, 'Discourse on the Theory of Only Consciousness' by Kuiji 窺基 (632–682 CE). T1830.43.0234b13.

Therefore the wholesomeness of a single thought for the great teachings can be known to requite the compassion of all the Buddhas in the ten directions. In theory it is exceeding rare, for it is like the Udumbara flower whose name occupies a unique position – to talk of it in glowing praise is similar then to fashioning ornamental accoutrements from gold. This is why the bodhisattvas elucidate the hidden meaning of the Mahayana. Listening to the not yet heard, it is capable of cutting through to the extremity of doubt to come to complete faith. Can the blessings of the Dharma be exhausted? The power of its merits is without limits, as it is said in the *Prajñaparamitā Sūtra*,

> Once more Kauśika[62]
> Granted all types of sentiency in *Jambudvīpa*[63]
> And suppose, in the four continents[64]
> There are all types of sentiency
> Suppose there are all types of sentiency
> In a thousand small chiliocosms[65]
> Suppose there are all kinds of sentiency
> In a thousand middling chiliocosms
> Suppose there are all kinds of sentiency
> In a thousand great chiliocosms
> Again, suppose as many kinds of sentiency everywhere
> As there are grains of sand in the River Ganges
> That all who have achieved peerless, perfect awakening
> Have come to no turning back (to irreversibility)
> Then in concert they all utter the same words:
> Now I am joyful and promptly testify
> To the peerless perfect awakening
> To help uproot, from sentient beings

[62] Of the family of Kuśika, the family name of Indra 因陀羅 when he took human form.

[63] 贍部洲 *shanbuzhou*, *Jambudvīpa*, mythical great continent south of Mt. Sumeru, the *axis mundi*.

[64] The four continents making up the world in Indian mythology, grouped around Mt. Sumeru.

[65] Mt. Sumeru and its four surrounding continents, eight seas, and a ring of iron mountains form one small world; a thousand of these form a small chiliocosm; a thousand of these small chiliocosms form a medium chiliocosm; a thousand of these form a great chiliocosm, which is one Buddha-world.

The sufferings of birth and death
Causing the attainment
Of the most excellent definitive peace

If there are sons and daughters of good families
For accomplishing this task
The book of the profound *Prajñaparamitā*
Is then a multitude of precious adornments
So make an offering with reverence
Venerate and extol it, offer it universally
Bestow it on all
Uphold, read and chant it
Causing an excellent penetrative insight
Suchness deeply appreciated
What do you think?
Are all these good sons and daughters
From these causal conditions?
Will they then acquire much merit?
Śakra Devānām-Indra asked,[66]
How many World Honoured One (Bhagavan)?
How many Well-gone (Sugata)?[67]
At that time the Buddha addressed Indra, saying
If there are good sons and good daughters
Reading the profound *Mahāprajñāpāramitā-Sūtra*
Many will be the precious adornments
Make offerings then with reverence
Venerate and extol it
To those among them
The bestowal is adapted to the individual
To uphold, read and chant it
Causing an excellent penetrative insight
Suchness deeply appreciated

[66] 天帝釋 *Tian Di shi*, Śakra Devānām-Indra, mighty lord of devas, a tutelary god of Buddhism; he is inferior to the *Brahma, Viṣṇu,* and *Śiva*. Like all the gods, he is considered inferior to a Buddha or any who have attained bodhi.

[67] One of ten epithets of a Buddha.

Taking the limitless gates
To the skilfully subtle textual meaning
Explained in broad detail
The meaning is discerned
Causing them full understanding
To impart instruction and teach the precepts
To give rise to diligent training
Good sons and good daughters
The merits obtained are abundant
Much more than previous ones
Being without number, without limit
They cannot be enumerated[68]

In the *Mahāparanirvāṇa-Sūtra*[69] the Buddha says,

> Good sons! Except for the icchantika,[70] the rest of sentient beings, having heard this sutra, can each and everyone create the causes and conditions for awakening. The radiant sound of the Dharma entering those hair follicles [**422c**] will assuredly attain supreme and perfect enlightenment.[71] Why? If people are capable of making offerings and venerating the innumerable Buddhas, then will they come to a hearing of the *Mahāparanirvāṇa-Sūtra*. A person poor in merit will therefore not be able to gain a hearing.[72]

Therefore know that to obtain a hearing of the [ancestral] source (宗), which is mirrored in (鏡) these records (錄) – the universal consciousness's ever abiding ultimate reality of the Dharma way – all [who have obtained a hearing] have formed a deep causal basis in times past, having been close to

---

68 大般若波羅蜜多經 *Da Bore Boluo Miduo Jing, Mahāprajñāpāramitā-Sūtra,* translated by Xuanzang 玄奘 from 660–663. T0220.05.0569c28.

69 大般涅槃經 *Da banniepan jing, Mahāparinirvāṇa-Sūtra,* translated by Dharmakṣema 曇無讖 (385–433 CE). T0374.12. 0417c11.

70 See Karashima, Seishi. 2007. 'Who were the icchantikas?' in *Annual Report of the International Research Institute for Advanced Buddhology*: 67–80.

71 阿耨多羅三藐三菩提 *anuttara-samyak-saṃbodhi.*

72 T0374.12.0417c15.

32

Buddha assemblies, a very great matter not springing from minor conditions. Had they not been perfumed by hearing, what would be the cause of happening upon [the teachings]? Again, as the Buddha told Kāśyapa in the *Mahāparanirvāṇa-Sūtra*,

> When all good sons and good daughters always focus attention (繫) on cultivating the thought (*xin*) of these two words, that Buddha is *ever present* – Kāśyapa, if there are good sons and good daughters cultivating [the thought of] these two words, it should be known that such persons will be in accord with what I practise, and they will come to the place I have arrived at.[73]

This is because [these] persons have faith in this Dharma; be they ordinary people or sages; they practise and maintain the middle way (契會) and that which abides in their midst is the abiding Buddha. Conduct is dignified; practice is in the footsteps of the Buddha's practice. The *Explanation of the Treatise on Mahayana* says,

> Those first who show a freedom from doubt and faith in the merit of entering the way, refers to sentient beings. After hearing of the profundity, sublimity and vast Dharma-gate teachings of this great Mahayana, they also do not fear or doubt it in their consciousness, neither do they falter, nor take it lightly and they also do not denigrate it, but give rise to a conscious determination, give rise to a resolute consciousness, to a consciousness of reverence, to a loving faithful consciousness. These persons should be known as true sons of the Buddha who do not cut off the seed of the Dharma, do not cut off the seed of monkhood, do not cut off the Buddha-seed but continue ceaselessly, always growing moment to moment without end into the future. Furthermore, by the prediction of future enlightenment given privately by all the Buddhas they are also protected by all the untold bodhisattvas. [74]

---

[73] T0374.12.0382b09.

[74] 釋摩訶衍論 *Shi Moheyan Lun*, 'Explanation of the Treatise on Mahayana' (7th – 8th cent.?), a commentary on the *Awakening of Faith*. T 1668.32.0667a28. See 'East Asian Apocryphal Scriptures: Their Origin and Role in the Development of Sinitic Buddhism,' Charles Muller in *Bulletin of Toyo Gakuen University*, vol. 6 (1998).

Therefore this treatise continues,

> Suppose that the persons who have already heard this Dharma do not become faint-hearted, then it can be seen (known) that these persons have certainly joined the lineage of the Buddhas and necessarily have received a prediction of enlightenment in the future from all the Buddhas.

The second comparison shows the superiority of the cure.

> This refers to persons capable of assimilating well and transforming the sentient beings pervading the three thousand great chiliocosms, all without any exceptions, to cause them to practise the ten wholesome behaviours.[75] Perhaps there are sentient beings who, in one instant during eating (一食頃), investigate and ponder this exceedingly profound Dharma. Comparing these two peoples' virtues, the merit that is obtained by the first kind is extremely small; the example is a mustard seed broken into one hundredth of a part. The merit this second kind of person obtains is extremely great. The example is crushing all the worlds in the ten directions into innumerable particles of dust.[76]

Therefore this treatise says,

> Suppose there were a person capable of transforming the sentient beings in three-thousand great chiliocosms, to have them practise the ten wholesome behaviours – that would not be as good as a person truly contemplating this Dharma in one instant of taking food, for this would surpass in merit the previous one; it is inconceivable.

The third [case]

> Concerning those who embrace and uphold the merit of and extol the teach-

---

[75] 十善 *shi shan*, the ten wholesome behaviours; not killing; not stealing; not committing adultery; not lying; not speaking harshly; not speaking divisively; not speaking idly; not being greedy, not being angry, not having wrong views.

[76] T1668.32.667b14.

ings, refers to people who embrace [**423a**] this commentary, contemplate and investigate its meaning and principle, be it for a day or a night, or the time in between. The power of the merits which have been obtained by them are immeasurable and boundless, indescribable and inconceivable. Suppose that all the Buddhas in the ten directions of the three worlds and all the bodhisattvas in the ten directions of the three worlds, with their tongues numerous as the motes of dust in all the ten directions of the three worlds, and that each and every [tongue], as numerous as the tiny motes of dust in the ten directions of the three worlds were totally conscious (悉) – this could not be described in aeons. Neither could the praise of these persons' merit which they have acquired be exhausted. Why is that? The merit of the Dharma-body as true thusness is coterminous with the realm of space; it is therefore without limit. What is more, could ordinary persons of the two vehicles praise it? One day and one night are not many, nor [the time] in between for a person to embrace it, yet the merit received is inconceivable. How much the more so if it were two days, if it were three days, if it were four days or even to a hundred days, to embrace, read and recite it, to ponder and investigate it – it cannot be conceived. It is the inexplicable within the inexplicable, which is why this treatise says that if people repeatedly embrace this treatise, investigate and practise it, even for one day and one night, the meritorious power accruing is without measure or limits – it cannot be explained. If all the Buddhas in the ten directions were each one, for a limitless, incalculably long aeon to praise its meritorious power, they would not be able to exhaust it. Why is that? It means that the meritorious power of the Dharma-nature is inexhaustible. Such a person's merit is also like this; there is no limit to it.[77]

Therefore, know that faith in this source teaching of consciousness (心宗), fulfils the Mahayana and is the same as what all the Buddhas of the three worlds have realised. How could its meaning and principle be exhausted? It is equally that which the bodhisattvas of the ten directions course in – the meritorious power is inexhaustible, an occasion for profound transformation, a rejoicing exceedingly deep. To obey the Buddha's transcendent teachings and then requite Buddha's compassion – there is no greater Dharma. To clarify the Buddha-sun and then open the Buddha-eye consists solely in clarifying consciousness (明心) within

---

this Ancestral Mirror (宗鏡). When a single phrase is attained to, the spirit is entered. It is a seed passing through the aeons, how much more profound is an impartial utterance, gathered in a collection of sutras – and this being one of a measureless number. When one is imbued with this Dharma, this is the seed of the perfect and sudden awakening, which can be called entering the summit of the sweet dew, the ghee irrigating consciousness, the lamp of non-dual wisdom shining. It destroys the delusive root of sentimentality by infusion of the single taste of the water of wisdom and rinses away the absurd defilements of one's objective opinions. It is able to bring about the transcendence of deeply obscured, thick hindrances, as when a fierce wind disperses hazardous foliage, the accumulated, stagnant doubts.

It is like a radiant sun's glitter on smooth ice, as if amongst all kings being king of the golden wheel, or amongst all luminaries being the shining light of the rising sun; amongst all treasures being the wish-fulfilling *mani* jewel; amongst all flowers being the blue flowering lotus; amongst all truths, being the gate to true emptiness; amongst all dharmas, being the abode of nirvana; therefore a gatha in the *Vajrasamādhi-Sūtra* says,

> The single taste of the Dharma-seal
> Is the accomplishment of the One Vehicle[78] [423b]

Amongst all sentient beings it is the ability to be a leader, a teacher, taking clarity as the guide, as the *Pravara-deva-rāja-paripṛcchā* says,

> Of all Dharma teachings
> Consciousness is supreme[79]

Mahāprajñāpāramitāśāstra says,

---

[78] 金剛三昧經 *Jingang sanmei jing, Vajrasamādhi-Sūtra,* T0273.09.0367b17. Possibly of Korean origin; see Buswell, Robert E., Jr. *The Formation of Ch'an Ideology in China and Korea* and *Cultivating Original Enlightenment.*

[79] 勝天王般若經 *Shengtianwang bore jing, Pravara-deva-rāja-paripṛcchā,* (勝天王般若波羅蜜經) translation by Upaśūnya/Ūrdhvaśūnya, 月婆首那 Indian, son of a king (565 CE). A Prajjnparamita text taught in Rajagrha to Pravara-deva-raja. T0231.08.0697c09.

All the Buddhas of the three worlds
Take the true reality of Dharma as teacher[80]

A patriarch said,

Among all insights, the bright penetration of consciousness is supreme[81]

A gatha in the *Fahua Jing* (Lotus Sutra) says,

The supreme guide
Has obtained this unexcelled Dharma[82]

Further, if the entry into the Ancestral Mirror [teachings] has yet to take place, it is not only that insight into the Way has not been obtained. The truth is that absolute (理) is the superlative [basis for] cultivation of the practice, so that with the root established, the path is born. The return to the root then is the ultimate, tantamount to contemplating the root nature. Although being familiar with the images [in pre/un-consciousness 本質][83] yet they are not real. If the nature of the storehouse consciousness were awoken to, the phenomenal world of objects would then be seen as illusory (妄). Therefore, a gatha in the sutra says,

It is not that thusness is not realised
But that one is able to awaken
To conditional phenomena as being mirages
They all appear to exist yet are not real[84]

---

80 大智度論 T1509.25.0128c28.

81 佛說須真天子經 *Xuzhentianzi jing, Suvikrāntacinti-devaputra-paripṛcchā*, 'Sutra of the Questions of Suvikrantacinti-devaputra', translation by Dharmarakṣa 竺法護 (239–316). T0588.15.0108c14.

82 T0262.09.0009c21.

83 本質 *ben zhi* – for the complexities of this term see Muller, DDB; also Dan Lusthaus, *Buddhist Phenomenology*, p. 14.

84 大方廣佛華嚴經隨疏演義鈔 *Dafangguang fo huayan jing suishu yanyi chao*, 'Sub-commentary and explanation of the meaning of the *Buddhâvataṃsaka-mahāvaipulya-Sūtra*' composed by Chengguan (澄觀, 738–839). T1736.36.0188c21.

Therefore, on attaining the root one comes to the ultimate, which is why Ocean of Realisation Bodhisattva in the *Huayan jing* makes use of the Dharma-realm samadhi to accord with the phenomenal world. And in the chapter on the appearance [of a Buddha in the world] (出現品) it is said,

> This Dharma-gate is called the hidden place of the Tathāgata, as well as being called the discourse on the fundamentally rooted true nature of the Tathāgata, an ultimately inconceivable Dharma.[85]

Thus the ancient worthy [Chengguan] said,

> When analysing (breaking down 剖) a chapter of a sutra from the phenomenal world, then thought after thought bears fruit. Exhausting the vow to benefit self and others is to fulfil the practice in all situations (塵塵).[86]

How could one believe in this text without having awoken to [the Buddhist teachings from] the Ancestral Mirror? If for a moment it is believed, the meritorious power is all present. Though what is practised will not be easy, when the Dharma-gate teachings are fully completed, it is exactly the blockages that are understood, precisely the wrong that is corrected; therefore a man of old times [Chengguan] said,

> Those who encounter this teaching should rejoice for themselves – like drowning in a vast ocean, then encountering a fragrant boat; fallen into a vast emptiness and finally riding on an immortal crane.[87]

423b18

Question: In general, to present and elucidate the great teaching in order to transform beings, it is necessary that one's own practice be completely accomplished by having passed through the stages of personal realisation; only then

---

[85] 大方廣佛華嚴經 *Dafangguangfo huayan jing, Buddhâvataṃsaka-mahāvaipulya-Sūtra,* translated by Buddhabhadra and others (418–420) in sixty fascicles. T0279.10.0277b24.

[86] 大方廣佛華嚴經疏 *Dafangguang fo huayan jing shu,* 'Commentary on the Flower Ornament Sutra' in 60 fasc., by Chengguan. T1735.35.0503b07.

[87] T1736.36.0014b07.

38

will the original vow have been fulfilled. Then to open the gate of expedient means is of benefit, not counterfeit, neither will it be at odds with the correct teachings. That which is recorded here, has it been clearly realised?

423b21

Answer: This [work] is merely a collection of words and teachings of the Buddhas, Patriarchs and Bodhisattvas, which is why it is called a record. The arrangement has questions and answers by way of exposition, all of which lean on a general summary of ancient worthies. Drawing on the praise for and encouragement to practise, it relates, in a complete manner, the authoritative teachings. Could one dare refer arbitrarily to an elucidation of the teachings? The presentation would be frivolous.

But again, the authoritative school of the Buddhas and Patriarchs is the true nature of 'Only Consciousness' (唯識). Everybody can be humanised just through faith. When discussing the gate to practice and realisation, everywhere it is said that [their] merit is not yet equal to all the sages. Moreover, within the teachings there is consensus, that it is comparable to the knowledge of newly fledged bodhisattvas, a promising concordance with the teachings, which are then understood. The initial entry is by faith on hearing and understanding; later the same is understood non-conceptually. If the entry is through the gate of faith, then the ascent is to the rank of a patriarch.

Now, having collected these [records from] the Ancestral Mirror, the process of verification will have no limits and they should be recollected with full penetration. It is all there to see.

Let us now confine the discussion to the affairs of the world within the realm of sentient beings. In the first place is [**423c**] knowledge by inference; the second is to know by appearances; the third is knowledge in accord with a doctrine.

As for knowledge by inference, it is as if the present body were being governed by nescience.[88] At night there are only dreams and within the dreams beautiful and ugly objects are seen, sadness and delight are vivid. Waking up on one's couch, dozing peacefully, how could these [dreams] ever have been [experienced] as real? Actually, it is just consciousness and thought working

---

[88] 有漏 *you lou*, āsrava, a condition associated with the state of nescience 無明, which allows the consciousnesses to be tricked by the illusions of subject and object, like and dislike.

within the dream; this then is the knowledge by inference. The things that were seen, at the time of waking up, were all unreal, as a dream.

The three worlds of past, present and future are primarily the intimately objective aspects of the [subjective] eighth consciousness of the *ālayavijñāna*. [All phenomena therein] are nothing but the ever changing activity of *ālaya* consciousness.[89] If there is an object present then it is revealed and discriminated in consciousness (意識 mentality *mano-vijñāna*)[90] (是明了意識分別) [as an object]. If the object cognised in past, present or future is thought about, it is the distracted, confused consciousness [of *mano-vijñāna*]. None of the objects of dream or waking consciousness, although different, are beyond consciousness, so that the gist of 'Only Consciousness'[91] is comparatively clear.

As to the second, to know by the appearance [of things], it is to clearly understand manifest phenomena at their face value and not dependent on hypotheses. Much like, for example, when seeing blue or white objects in the present; the object itself is inherently empty, does not say 'I am blue', 'I am white'. It is all a matter of visual consciousness seeing a part of its own nature, subjectively differentiating the [object] spontaneously, whilst, at the same time, it is clearly revealed in awareness (consciousness). Discursive thought calculates whether it is blue or white.[92] By distinguishing its colour mentally (以意辯), language is used to designate it as blue, all this established as inherently false verbal expression. Moreover, by virtue of the six dusts (senses) being blunted, they are not self-existent (independent) essences, and do not call themselves by name.

Since colours are like this, all phenomena (法) are thus, for nothing has a self-nature; all is verbal construct. Therefore it is said that all phenomena are originally inactive (本閑) but that people trouble themselves and on this account give occasion for consciousness to arise and for the existence of all the objective realms. However, if the place of arising is an empty consciousness, then the objective realms are all empty; thus, emptiness is not empty of/in itself

---

[89] 本識 *ben shi*, an early term for *ālayavijñāna*.

[90] The sixth of the eight consciousnesses in Yogacara, a form of conscious awareness like the five sense organs, whereas the eighth, *ālayavijñāna* and seventh, *manas* constitute the subconscious regions of consciousness.

[91] 唯心 *wei xin* – only consciousness – all perception of phenomena is produced by consciousness.

[92] 計度分別 *jidu fenbie*, to conceptualise about various matters in past, present and future.

40

but is due to consciousness being empty. Existence is not existent of/in itself but is due to consciousness existing. Since it is neither, empty nor existent, then it is 'Only Consciousness,' only heart (唯識唯心). Were there to be no-thing in consciousness, all phenomena would be peacefully stable (安寄). Similarly with objects of the past – could they ever have been? Wherever a thought arises, then suddenly it is present. If thoughts were not to arise, no perceptual objects would ever appear. All this is the daily functioning of sentient beings, who can clearly understand without waiting to accomplish it. How could it be attained by cultivation? Anyone with consciousness can prove it completely. Therefore, an ancient worthy said that if there were a person with great root faculties knowing that it is only consciousness constantly scrutinising (觀) its own consciousness and then consciously naming the object, this is the beginning period of contemplation/observation (觀). Although he has not yet become a sage, if [the object] is clearly acknowledged by its conscious expression, then this is a bodhisattva.

As for the third, knowledge that is in accord with doctrine, a sutra says, 'The three worlds are 'Only Consciousness' (唯識), the ten thousand dharmas only heart (唯心)'[93] – this is the realisation of the original principle (本理), able to elucidate [the transmission of] the true teachings (正宗) in detail, as [stated] below. As the *Chenshi lun* says, 'It proves there is not [only] one [resolve to attain bodhi].'[94]

[In the *Huayanjing tanxuan ji* it says],

> The Buddha spoke words of the inside, outside, the middle and in between, then entered samadhi. At that time there were five hundred Arhats present and each interpreted these words. After the Buddha emerged from samadhi all questioned the Bhagavan. 'To whom do the Buddha's teachings apply (誰當佛意)?' The Buddha said, 'They are not really my [424a] teachings.' Again they questioned the Buddha, 'Since it does not serve as the Buddha's [personal] teachings, they will not offend.' The Buddha said, 'Although not

---

93 大方廣佛華嚴經 *Dafangguangfo huayan jing, Buddhâvataṃsaka-mahāvaipulya-Sūtra*, translated by Buddhabhadra and others (418–420) in sixty fascicles. T0279.10.0288c05.

94 成唯識論 *Cheng weishi lun,* 'Discourse on the Theory of Only Consciousness'. T1585.31.0008a29.

my teachings, each one conforms to the correct principle and is worthy of being a sagely principle, of good fortune, without faults.'[95]

It is also the same as the teachings of the lesser vehicle's self-validation of the Dharma-gates, which are still in accordance with the correct principle; how much the more so when wholly guided by the One Vehicle. Is this only chatter about the Buddha's aims? The *Six Practises of the Dharma*[96] says, 'All those of great wisdom who desire to train in the Way do not ask about the greater or lesser [vehicle] for all rely on the principle of the teachings.' If insight were gained into the expedient (權) teachings and even if it were taught by the Buddha, if it were not acknowledged to be the real word, then it would not be complied with. If one sees an average man talking of the existence of principle, although it is not the Buddha word, still it is relied on for practice, because there are those who possess wisdom and train in the Buddha-dharma and understand the Tathāgata well. The teachings are [both] expedient and true and rely on the Buddha's teaching of reality by proclaiming the principles of the Way, so it is beyond the foolish who mistakenly [only] grasp at the expedient.

Therefore, if a wise person has something to say, even if it is an average person, the Dharma teaching is, in that case, the same as the Buddha's. It is like a pitcher conveying water. Pouring the water into another pitcher, although the pitcher is different, the water is the same. So too, although the average person's fetters of affliction have yet to be exhausted, it does not hinder a person's understanding. They are able to talk of the true meaning (實義) as long as their mental faculty comprehends the principle.

To ponder, this is the first contemplation of principle, but different from other worldly people. If it is called pondering on man's emptiness, then it refers to the two vehicles. When contemplation is on the emptiness of Dharma, this then is the bodhisattva. So the *She lun* says, 'First practise contemplation, this then is a worldling bodhisattva.'[97] With the evidence of these scriptures begin-

---

[95] 華嚴經探玄記 *Huayanjing tanxuan ji*, 'Record of the Search for the Profundities of the Huayan *Sutra*' by Fazang 法藏 (643–712). T1733.35.0111c01.

[96] 六行法 T48.424a04. Source unknown. Perhaps the six paramitas – charity, morality, forbearance, effort, meditation and wisdom?

[97] 攝論 *Shè lùn Mahāyāna-saṃgraha-bhāṣya* (攝大乘論釋), 'Commentary to the summary of the Great Vehicle' ascribed to Asaṅga, 無著 translation by Paramārtha 眞諦 (499–569). T1595.31.0174c07.

42

ners contemplate them. Although the fetters have not yet been cut, still they are bodhisattvas by virtue of being able to understand the principle, the same as the great sages, for what is said then is in harmony with the principle. Each one can rely on the other. The *Jewel Box sutra* says,

> It is like the Kalaviṅka bird's[98] offspring in the egg – it pecks before being born and produces the wonderful sound of the Kalaviṅka bird. In the egg of the Buddha-dharma are all bodhisattvas. Although the view of self is not yet destroyed, nor have the three realms been left, nevertheless, they are able to produce the wonderful sound of the Buddha's Dharma. It is referred to as the empty, signless, uncreated activity of the sound of the Kalaviṅka bird. If it goes to a muster of peacocks[99] it never sings but still when it returns among the Kalaviṅka then it needs must sing. If the bodhisattva comes to all the sravakas and pratyekabuddhas, ultimately he does not elucidate the unfathomable Dharma of the Buddhas; but when he comes to the assembly of the bodhisattvas then he explains the teachings to them.[100]

This text is the proof of it. In the worldly stage, although faults have not yet been exhausted, it does not hinder deep understanding. As for talk of the existence of the principle, all may believe and accept it. But all worldly people who talk of the existence of principle have practised in a former life; they are not beginners now. If it is not [due to] former life practice, then the present training has come of age, only expressed in other words.

From still being confused about the principle and due to this confusion over principle, despite coming out with many words, the expedient and the true (the temporal and the real) are not yet understood, so in this case speech is contrary to principle. If the principle were understood, there would be no distinction made between a sage and a non-sage (child 幼).

To simply seek the Way, not to seek phenomenal things, is to rely on the

---

98 An immortal bird in Buddhism, it has a human head, a bird's torso and long a flowing tail. The *kalaviṅka* dwells in the Western Pure Land (西方淨土 *Sukhāvatī*; Blissful) and preaches the Dharma with its fine voice, sings while still un-hatched with a voice like the Buddha's voice.

99 Peacocks or peafowl do not mix well with other [domestic] birds.

100 寶篋經 (無字寶篋經) *Baoqie jing,* T828. This is actually from 大方廣寶篋經 'The Great and broad (*vaipulya*) Jewel Box Sutra'. T0462.14.0468b25.

Dharma, not to rely on man. As with Aśvajit; it was because Śāriputra saw him pursuing the Dharma that he then replied in verse [to Śāriputra's questioning],[101]

> My years [in the sangha] are immature [**424b**]
> The days of learning also shallow
> How to proclaim the ultimate truth
> To extensively expound theTathāgata's teachings?[102]

Śāriputra replied that the essentials could be related briefly. Then [Aśvajit] recited another gatha,

> All dharmas arise from causes and conditions
> These dharmas are explained as causes and conditions
> These dharmas are the cessation of causes and conditions
> Thus the great teacher explains[103]
> 諸法因緣生 是法說因緣 是法因緣盡 大師如是說
>
> *[Those dharmas which arise from a cause*
> *The Tathāgata has declared their cause*
> *And that which is the cessation of them*
> *Thus the great Renunciant has taught]*[104]

As soon as Śāriputra heard this gatha he attained the first fruit[105] and trans-

---

[101] 阿濕婆恃 Aśvajit (Pali: Assaji Thera). Name of the fifth of the *Pañcavaggiya* monks and a relative of Śākyamuni: he was responsible for the conversion of Śāriputra and Moggallāna. DPPN: I, 224.

[102] 中本起經 *Zhong benqi jing*, 'The Sutra on the Origin-middle Part', translation by Tan-guo 曇果 and Kang Mengxiang 康孟詳, 12th year of Jian'an 建安, Eastern Han 東漢 (207CE). Translated into Dutch by Erik Zürcher, *Het leven van de Boeddha : Xiuxing Benqi jing & Zhong benqi jing*.

[103] *Dizhidu lun*, T1509.25.0136c04.

[104] Translation after the Pali by Boucher, Daniel. 1991. 'The Pratītyasamutpādagāthā and its role in the medieval cult of the relics', *Journal of the International Association of Buddhist Studies* 1991, 14: 1–27; there are various early Chinese translations of this well-loved verse, T186; 192; 196; 200. DPPN: I.224.

[105] The stage of *srota-āpanna* 預流果, illusion discarded and the stream of enlightenment entered.

mitted the teaching to Maudgalyāyana,[106] which, on being repeated, he [too] attained the Way [of the first fruit].

By these means realisation is attested. Wise people seek the Dharma and only give weight to the virtue of others, are not shamed by being a follower and are not the same as the foolish who are sluggish and arrogant. Although [the foolish] acknowledge the superiority of others, they are ashamed and not willing to learn. Average people who do not begin cannot enter the Way; because of this very many are incapable of searching for the Dharma. So all the foolish must be confused about the teaching on reality and have not yet been able to awaken to themselves. They should only visit the virtuous, for, on account of being confused about the principle, even whilst possessing worldly wisdom, in the absence of a friend of the Way confusion over the Way will ever persist. As the *Pravara-deva-rāja-paripṛcchā Sūtra* says,

> It is like being born blind, unable to see forms; thus sentient beings afflicted with blindness cannot gain insight into the Dharma; like people who have eyes but no light from the outside penetrates. [Those] practitioners of the Way are like this – unable to see form even in the possession of wisdom; so if a virtuous friend of the Way is not present there is no capacity for insight into the Dharma. [107]

By this means realisation is attested. Even when people are wise, they have not yet been able to awaken to themselves – a good friend is needed. This is why the *Transmission of the Dharma Treasure Sutra* says, 'A good Dharma-friend is really a complete set of causes and conditions for attaining the Way.'[108] The Buddha himself urges people to seek after a good Dharma-friend and to be careful not to pay court to the foolish. A whole lifetime passed in vain is the reason why all the Buddhas have bequeathed profound teachings, which cause reliance on the Dharma exclusively, not on man; to rely on the meaning rather than relying on words. The bodhisattva might still transform the body into an

---

[106] One of the ten principal disciples of Śākyamuni. See 目犍連. (Pāli Mahā-moggallāna). See DPPN: II.541.

[107] T0231.08.0719c20

[108] 付法藏因緣傳 *Fu fazang Yinyuan Zhuan*, 'Chronicle of the Successive Transmission of the Dharma Canon' circa 472 CE? (DDB). T2058.50.0322a25.

animal or discourse on the Dharma for the sake of humans – [but] appearances such as these are rare.

By causing listeners to receive [the teachings] with faith, so that all shall be awakened to the Way and have them enter the Dharma of universal equality,[109] how then could that cause consciousness to give rise to [feelings of] superiority or inferiority? Thus [Chengguan's sub-commentary to the *Buddhâvataṃsaka-mahāvaipulya-Sūtra*],

> [Has] Nan saying (?),[110] that these pointers are subtle and mysterious and 'are only realised at the highest stage, so how can ordinary feelings get a glimpse of the great teachings?' The explanation is that by relying on the principle of the teachings, the teachings of the sages are endorsed. The *Nirvāṇa Sūtra* says, 'The totally fettered average person is able to know the Tathāgata's hidden treasury,' and a gatha in the *Mahāvairocanābhisaṃbodhi Sūtra* says, 'It is due to the sun shining brightly that the wheel of the sun is seen and by the bright rays of the Buddha's wisdom that one sees the Way practised by the Buddha. Therefore the Buddha's teaching is an understandable teaching.'[111]

Now, from beginning to end the Ancestral Mirror draws in the light of the Buddha's wisdom teachings and shows forth the course that the Buddha practised. If there is deep faith, then this is on account of sentient beings' light of consciousness, of insight into sentient beings' path of conduct. Therefore Nan says that ordinary people, who are not in harmony with those who know, that such and such a person only has mistaken views, do not have faith. So the *Mahāsaṃgha-Sūtra* says

> If there is a person who says 'I am excellent and the Buddha is excellent,' (我異佛異) then it should be known that this person is a disciple of Mara.[112]

---

[109] A key teaching of the *Prajñaparamitā* literature, as is the in-depth appraisal of the equality of all things/dharmas (平等性智) due to the realisation of emptiness.

[110] Ananda's dialogue in one of the sutras cited in T1736?

[111] Chengguan's sub-commentary, wherein he quotes from the *Huayan Jing*, the *Nirvāṇa Sūtra* and the *Mahāvairocanābhisaṃbodhi Sūtra*. T1736.36.0039a16.

[112] 大集經 *Daji jing Mahāsamnipāta-Sūtra*, 'Great Collection Sutra' translated by Dharmakṣema 曇無懺 (385–433 CE) and others. T0397.13.0089a14.

46

It is also said that those with penetrative insight know that all dharmas are without the characteristic of duality. Also, that 'those contemplating the dharmas are referred to as Buddhas.'[113]

Therefore [424c] a student asked Imperial Preceptor [Hui]Zhong,

'The Tathāgata discourses on *prajñā*, which is not [discoursing on] *prajñā*,'[114] this is called *prajñā*. Now that right and wrong have been exhausted, then say what is *prajñā*? Answer: The one who can understand that it is not a name, this is *prajñā*.
Question: Does the Buddha also elucidate it like this?
Answer: There is no difference between the ancients and moderns. This being the case, a thousand Buddhas are of the same consciousness; the ten thousand sages on the same track.[115]

424c05

Question: The gate to the teachings of expedient means of all the Buddhas relies on promoting (起) the root capacities of living beings. But root natures vary; dharmas are only dust and sand. The thirty-seven factors of enlighten-

---

[113] T0397.13.0086b02.

[114] 金剛般若波羅蜜經 *Vajracchedikā prajñāpāramitāSūtra,* 'Diamand Sutra', translation by Paramātha 真諦 (499–569). T0237.08.0763c18. For the extended entries on Huizhong in the CDL see T2076.244a07; ibid:, 437c17, which contains oral teachings (RTL: 5.98 & 28.1). See also YYCC:78–81 & 147–151 and notes.

[115] T48.0424c01. This passage is also translated in YYCC: 163. Yanshou's source[s] for Chan master Huizhong (†775), an eminent master of the Tang dynasty, are unknown. But, 'The existence of a record of Huizhong's teachings is confirmed in the records of the Japanese monk Enchin 円珍 (814–891) [...] called the Enchin mokuroku 円珍目録. In Enchin's catalogue, there appears a title purporting to be the teachings of Huizhong, the Nanyang [Hui]zhong heshang yanjiao 南陽忠和尚言教 (The Oral Teachings of Reverend Nanyang Huizhong). This is the likely source from which Yanshou drew his material on Huizhong in the ZJL.' YYCC: 148 & n.34, p. 304. (日本比丘圓珍入唐求法目録 T2172.55.1101a27: 南陽忠和上言教一本).

ment[116] aid the entry to the Way, the fifty-two stages[117] are the path of cultivating practice. So why posit only one consciousness as being the Ancestral Mirror [teachings]?

424c08

Answer: This absolute reality (法) of the universal consciousness (一心) is principle (noumenon) and phenomena in complete [union]; it is the father of great compassion, the mother of *prajñā* (wisdom), the precious treasury of the Dharma, the origin of the ten thousand practises. By virtue of all the Dharma realms, all the Buddhas of the ten directions, all the mahasattvas, pratyeka-buddha and sravakas, all sentient beings, each and all have this universal con-sciousness in common. All the Buddhas have all already awakened to this, whilst living beings do not know it. Now, for the sake of those who do not know, the expedient means [of the Buddhas] indicate it unswervingly (直指). Since [consciousness] is an innate possession, it is not false; because it is reachable, it is not fallacious, which is why a gatha in the *Huayan Jing* says,

> It is like a person in the world
> Hearing of the existence of a treasure trove
> Because it may be reachable
> Consciousness gives rise to great joy[118]

The location of the treasure trove is in the consciousness of living beings, at the moment of entering the gate of faith, it appears quite naturally. Then it is realised that they are fully endowed with it from the beginning. How could this be merely a nominal advantage (假功成)? The beginning of knowing that the original nature is without distinctions is not come to through practice. This could be called the most efficacious (最靈) in worldly affairs, the origin of the

---

[116] 三十七道品 sanshiqi daopin, saptatriṃśad-bodhi-pakṣikā-dharmāḥ, 'The thirty-seven factors of enlightenment.' They are the four bases of mindfulness 四念處, the four kinds of right effort 四正勤, the four transcendental powers 四神足, the five whole-some roots 五根, the five powers 五力, the seven factors of enlightenment 七覺支, and the eightfold holy path. See Étienne Lamotte, *Le traité de la grande vertu de sagesse,* Tome III. Louvain: pp. 1119–1137.

[117] The fifty-two stages on the path of the bodhisattva, well known in the teaching of the *Huayan jing* (Avatamsaka Sutra) and others works.

[118] T0278.09.0583a21.

48

ultimate path, the ineffable gate. Its essential and real meaning is that the root origin of ordinary people and sages be regarded as the fundamental cause of delusion and awakening; all things come to their ground [of being] and prosper. The realisation of principle is all practices accomplished. All the disciplines are a vigorous entry, all the strength of irreproachable conduct (德) returns and serves as the foundation for a thousand sages to pursue the Way, being the eye of all the Buddhas who appear in the world. Therefore, if awakened to one's own consciousness, it suddenly becomes Buddha wisdom, which can be called the meeting of a hundred rivers in the one source (一濕); modelling a multitude of dust particles to make one ball; smelting rings and bracelets to form one piece of gold or changing sweet cream into the single taste. As a gatha in the *Huayan Jing* has it, 'Unable to awaken to one's own consciousness / how could one know the Buddha-nature?'[119] As the *Akṣayamati Pusa Jing* says, 'Just correct one's own consciousness, do not pursue another training.'[120] And *The Sutra on the Essentials of Meditation* says, 'Illumination within opens up liberation / this is the teaching of the great vehicle.'[121] Insight into one's own nature of consciousness is referred to as illumination. The journey which the multitude of sages makes is called entering the gate. A gatha in the *Laṅkāvatāra-Sūtra* says,

> Consciousness is fully endowed with the Dharma treasure
> Free from the stain of the view of an 'I'
> The World-honoured One discourses on all practices
> The Dharma that is known is within consciousness[122]

---

[119] T0279.10.0082a26.

[120] 阿差末菩薩經 *Achamo pusajing* (*Akṣayamati Pusa Jing*), 'The Sutra of Bodhisattva Akṣayamati' (T403.13 [no. 39 (12)], translated by Tripitaka master Dharmarakṣa 三藏 竺法護 (239–316 CE) of 西晉 Western Jin. Master Yanshou's quotation is not found in this sutra.

[121] 禪要經 *Chanyao Jing*, 'Sutra on the Essentials of Meditation' translator unknown: Eastern Han period (25–220 CE). This quotation is not in T609, nor in T616. It is in 小 室六門 'Xiaoshi's Six Gates' (T 2009.48.0370c27), a collection of six treatises attributed to Bodhidharma, earliest extant edition is dated 1647 from Tokugawa Japan. The individual treatises of which it is composed, however, were written in China during the Tang 唐代 (618–907). Muller, DDB.

[122] 入楞伽經 *Renlengjia jing*, *Laṅkāvatāra-Sūtra*, 'Sutra on (the Buddha's) Entering (the Country of) Lanka' translated by Bodhiruci 菩提流支 (? –527 CE). T0671.16.0515a17.

A gatha in the *Candrapradīpa-samādhi-Sūtra* says,

> If there is a reception and retaining of this One Dharma
> One can follow the correct practice of the bodhisattva
> Due to the meritorious power of this One Dharma
> The unsurpassed Way will be quick of attainment[123]

The Śrīmālādevīsiṃhanāda-*Sūtra* says,

> World-honoured One! I have seen into and retained the true Dharma; having this great power, the Tathāgata, [**425a**] with this as the eye, is the root origin of the Dharma, is the guide into the Dharma, is the penetration of the Dharma.[124]

The explanation is that what is named as the True Dharma is the supreme impulse of consciousness (義心). Consciousness outside, of deluded projections, seeking something outside of principle, will fall completely into a one-sided error. Therefore, [when] confused about correct insight, gain the true eye of the Tathāgata. Assimilated completely, to the limits of the ten directions, it will illumine the very limits of the Dharma realm and return all to the universal consciousness – this is called taking in and receiving the true Dharma. The *Awakening of Faith* says,

> Furthermore, the intrinsic nature and characteristic of *thusness* is that all worldlings, sravakas, pratyekabuddhas, bodhisattvas and Buddhas are without its increase or decrease. There is no arising [of it] in a former life, no cessation in an afterlife but is a ceaselessly consummating realisation (常恒究竟). From beginningless time the original nature is fully endowed with meritorious power (功德), which means it brightly emanates great

---

[123] 月燈三昧經 *Yuedeng sanmei jing,* 'The Discourse to Prince Candraprabha' a text on meditation, translated by Narêndrayaśas 那連提耶舍 (517–589 CE) in 557. T0639.15.0549b19.

[124] 勝鬘經 *Shemgman Jing,* (勝鬘師子吼一乘大方便方廣經) *Śrīmālādevī-simha-nāda-Sūtra,* translated into Chinese in 436 CE by Guṇabhadra 求那跋陀羅 (394–468) T353. See Wayman, Alex, and Hideko Wayman, trans. *The Lion's Roar of Queen Śrīmālā.* The literal quote is actually from the 大寶積經 *Da baoji jing Mahāratnakūṭa-Sūtra,* translated by Bodhiruci. T0310.11.0674c13.

wisdom, meaning, a universal illumining from the Dharma-realm, meaning, a true and full realisation, the original nature of the pristine consciousness, of permanence, bliss, self and purity,[125] it means quiescence, unchanging and unimpeded (自在) – such is [the intrinsic nature and characteristic of *thusness*], more [replete] than the grains of sand in the Ganges River. It is neither the same nor different for the Buddha-dharma is inconceivable, not discontinuous and because this is the meaning it is called the *tathāgatagharba*, also called the Dharma-body.[126]

425a12

Question: (Continuing the quote from T1667) Above it is said that *thusness* is far from all characteristics, so how can it now be said to be fully endowed with the characteristics of merit-producing power?

425a13

Answer: Although truly endowed with all meritorious power, nevertheless, it has no distinctive characteristics, for these dharmas are all the same – single in taste, single in truth and free from imaginary characteristics; therefore [*thusness*] has no dual nature. On account of relying on the characteristics of arising and ceasing of the karmic consciousnesses, all these distinctive characteristics are then set up. How is this established? By means of all dharmas – originally only consciousness (唯心). Truly, there is nothing to discriminate, but due to not being awakened, discrimination arises in consciousness.

To perceive that there is a world of objects is called nescience. The nature of consciousness is intrinsic purity (心性本淨); nescience does not arise [there] so it is called *thusness*. It means that the luminous great wisdom is established. If consciousness gives rise to perceiving objects, then this is the characteristic of not perceiving [*thusness*]. Since the nature of consciousness does not perceive [objects separate from *thusness*], there is then nothing not perceived, which is *thusness*. It means that the bright Dharma-

---

[125] The four virtuous aspects of realization 果德 taught in the Nirvana Sutra 涅槃經. These are taught as a positive response to the long-promulgated basic Buddhist notions of impermanence 無常, suffering 苦, no-self 無我, and defilement 污, which are taken to be four pitfalls 四顛倒.

[126] T1667.32.0587b16.

51

realm is everywhere established. If consciousness wavers, then it is not recognising reality, is not the purity of the original nature, neither is it permanence, bliss, self and purity, nor quiescence. It would be changeable, not free and because of this, defilements and delusion would arise more numerous than the grains of sand in the River Ganges.

If therefore the nature of consciousness is without movement, then the meaning of true realisation is established, the meaning being that the characteristics of merit-producing power even exceeds all the sands of the River Ganges. Since consciousness is subject to arising and perceives various objects, differentiates and seeks them out, then there is a deficiency in the laws within [consciousness] (內法). Therefore, the merit-producing power of no limits is precisely the universal consciousness's own nature and not to perceive various objects that could be sought [outside of *thusness*] is therefore the completeness exceeding the grains of sand in the River Ganges. It is neither the same, nor different, inconceivable, the Dharma of all the Buddhas, without there being any discontinuity; therefore it is called the *thusness* of the *tathāgatagharba*, also referred to as the Dharma body of the Tathāgata. [127]

Being so, this one (universal) consciousness is not like that of worldlings, [**425b**] who absurdly regard consciousness as capable of being deduced from conditions and grasp with certitude that it is [all] in the physical body. Now, in all the ten directions of the worldly realm, all is the ineffable lucency of the true consciousness of *thusness,* as the chapter on *Entering the Dharma-realm* of the *Avatamsaka Sutra* says,

In the world ocean of the Lotus Treasury there are no questions on whether there are mountains or rivers, for the great earth is empty; grass, trees and forests, dust particles and hairs, there is nothing that is not connected, referred to as the realm of the True Dharma, all endowed with unending power. [128]

---

[127] The more popular translation of Aśvaghoṣa's 馬鳴 work (T1666) is attributed to Paramārtha 眞諦 (499–569), while the later translation (T1667) is attributed to Śikṣānanda 實叉難陀 (arrived in China 694 CE). T1667.32.0587b16.

[128] 修華嚴奧旨妄盡還源觀 *Xiu huayan aozhi wangjinhuanyuan guan,* 'The Contempla-

Therefore an ancient worthy said,

> The [four] virtues of the *qian* hexagram are primal beginning, penetration, harmony and correctness.[129] It begins with primordial *qi* (一氣). Permanence, bliss, self and purity is the innate power of the Buddhas. The origin is in the one (universal) consciousness. Focussing on the primordial *qi* makes for suppleness; cultivating the one consciousness completes the Dao. As for consciousness, it is sublimely empty, pure subtlety, splendid iridescence, spiritual numinosity, without coming, without going, imperceptibly penetrating (冥通) past, present and future, neither inside nor outside, serenely pervasive, neither ceasing to be nor coming to be. How could the four mountains[130] be troubled? Free of nature, free of characteristics, how could the five colours be able to blind them?[131] Dwelling in the stream of birth and death, the dragon's pearl alone shines in the grey-blue ocean deep. Squatting by the shore of nirvana, the cinnamon disk[132] shines solitary in the blue-green heaven. Great indeed! All things owe their beginning to it.[133] All things are deceptive, coming together from various conditions; the arising of dharmas is originally non-arising, everything is only consciousness and consciousness is like a mirage, for there is only the one (universal, primordial) consciousness. [When] consciousness is quiescent, then it is known. The eye's perfect awakening is completely submerged in purity and does not contain other [elements] in its midst, therefore its innate power functions without limits. All is of one and the same (universal) nature. Characteristics arise from the original nature. Objects and cogni-

tion of the Profound Pointers of the *Huayan* Practice of Definitively Returning Delusion to the Source' by Fazang 法藏 (643–712).T1876.45.0637c27.

[129] 元亨利貞 *yuan, heng, li, zhen*, the hexagram *Qian* (乾卦) in the Book of Changes (周易), has been interpreted differently over the centuries: pure *yang* can naturally give birth to all things, 元 *yuan* beginnings; 亨 *heng* harmonises, 利 *li* benefits; 貞 *zhen* purifies. Also, benevolence, propriety, righteousness and justice; or the four seasons. Zongmi is perhaps quoting from Zixia (Bu Shang 卜商 507–400 BCE) Yizhuan 子夏易傳, juan I.

[130] Like four closing-in mountains are birth, age, sickness, and death. DCBT: 174.

[131] Various 'coloured' ideas. DCBT: 125.

[132] *Guilun* 桂輪 – the full moon, a symbol of perfect awakening.

[133] Zongmi quoting 周易 乾 – 大哉乾元萬物資始乃統天 'Vast is the primal beginning of *qian*! All things owe their beginning to it, uniting all of heaven.'

tion being present, characteristics attain fusion with the original nature. Consciousness and body are vast,[134] the place of the ocean-seal, beyond the great void. Be prepared for it, it dazzles, is far beyond any superficial conceptions. [135]

Indeed, a former worthy has said, that concerning the *tathāgatagharba*, it is a different name for the universal consciousness. Why is it referred to as one (universal) consciousness? It refers to the non-dual nature of all dharmas, true, false, defiled or pure; that is why it is called *one*, for there is no duality in this. It is the reality within all dharmas (phenomena), not the same as space; it is original sentient understanding (性自神解 or, spiritually awakened to the origin), therefore it is called consciousness.

If therefore the search is directed otherwise, to the outside through erroneous teachings, it would be like drilling in ice to search for fire or crushing pebbles to extract oil. Since there is no direct causal relationship between ice and fire, pebbles and oil, then wishing to seek a way of manipulating these is a fruitless expenditure of energy.

Furthermore, solely cultivating gradual practice is to abide in the emptiness of the expedient vehicle (空住權乘), which is like paint without glue, like unbaked bricks not yet fired, like firing a painting on a vessel not yet solid. As for the desire to search for the ultimate, there is no such place, but if one can truly penetrate one's own consciousness and not erroneously seek it outside, then it is like fire emerging from wood. From hemp comes oil, it does not violate the primary cause and so is speedily and successfully dealt with. Similarly of paint with glue; like unbaked clay passing through fire it would be capable of serving as a vessel, it is not a useless thing.

Whenever there are things to do, all is completely realised. If there is no deep faith yet, grasping and rejecting innumerable things, [then] following objects gives rise to delusions, to the harm of dharmas. Not to [actively] contemplate emptiness in order to dispatch lassitude, only grasping vacuity, the good is abandoned without giving rise to compassion. [425c] Only being attached to existence then gives rise to faults; it is all due to not comprehend-

---

[134] 相得性融身心廓爾. T48.0425b15.

[135] 大方廣圓覺修多羅了義經略疏註 *Dafangguang yuanjue xiuduoluo liaoyi jing lue-shuzhu,* 'An Abridged Commentary to the Sutra of Perfect Enlightenment' by Zongmi 宗密 (780–841). T1795.39.0524a16.

ing emptiness as the existence of the universal consciousness. This results in gain and loss. If the Ancestral Mirror teaching (宗鏡) were to be entered by an actual timely arousal of consciousness, not only would practice be accomplished, principle immediately completed, but one would then be the same as the ancient Buddhas, there being no difference between the mundane and the supra-mundane realms. As it is said in the *Mahāparanirvāṇa-Sūtra*, [136]

> In the city of Kuśinagara was a *caṇḍāla* (untouchable) by the name of Joy. The Buddha predicted that this person, from a single arousal of consciousness, would, whilst in this era of a thousand Buddhas, quickly achieve the unsurpassed true enlightenment.[137]

The *Fahua Xuanyi* says,

> As for consciousness itself (心法), it is a teaching that has already been clarified, so how could there be a different consciousness? It is only that the Dharma of sentient beings is extremely broad, the Buddha-dharma extremely lofty, difficult to study in the beginning. Nevertheless, consciousness, Buddha and sentient beings are not three different things. Merely by the self reflection on one's own consciousness, then it becomes easy. The *Nirvāṇa Sūtra* says, 'All sentient beings are fully endowed with the three samadhis.'[138] The highest samadhi is referred to as the Buddha-nature – the capacity to contemplate the nature of consciousness being the highest samadhi. The higher can unite with the lower, which is to assimilate the Dharma of sentient beings.' The *Huayan Sūtra* says, 'To saunter through the realm of consciousness itself (心法) is like [sauntering through] empty space, then all the Buddha-realms are known; the Dharma-realm is the middle. Space is emptiness; consciousness and Buddha are nominal designations. The three kinds are just the Buddha-realm. This is the contemplative consciousness, the ever fully endowed Buddha-dharma. Furthermore, consciousness sauntering through the Dharma-realm contemplates the dichotomy between the sense organs and their objective world. A moment

---

[136] 大般涅槃經 *Da banniepan jing, Mahāparinirvāṇa-Sūtra,* 'Sutra of the Great Decease' translated by Huiyan 慧嚴 (363–443). T0375.12.0664b24.

[137] 無上正眞[之]道 One of the Chinese translations for *anuttarā-samyak-saṃbodhi.*

[138] The samadhi of emptiness, of no-marks, of non-contrivance.

of cognition arising in consciousness [concerning] the ten elements[139] necessarily belongs to one [of these] elements. Even if it belongs to a single element, it nevertheless contains a hundred elements/realms, a thousand dharmas. In a single moment of cognition all these are complete[ly present]. This consciousness is a master of deception/shape shifter. In a single day and night it ceaselessly creates all kinds of living beings, each of the five aggregates, all kinds of lands, so-called hell-realms, countries fictitious or real, even Buddha-realms. Whether lands are fictitious or real, practitioners should choose for themselves which path they are able to follow.

Again, it is like empty space, consciousness is born from contemplating consciousness, without having to rely on conditions, consciousness [just] is. Consciousness is without the power to arise, conditions too are without arising. Consciousness and [causal] conditions are names, they do not exist. How could a union come about [between them]? Rather, union cannot be obtained. Separated then they do not arise, so that there is not even a single arising, so how could there be a hundred realms, a thousand dharmas? Since consciousness is empty, all that arises from consciousness is empty. This emptiness is also empty. Suppose empty were not empty, or a little bit empty, suppose it is a designation, the designation is also not a designation, it is neither designation nor is it empty: ultimate purity.[140]

Could it just be [about] the three contemplations?[141] The ten thousand practices, even as far as the ten directions of space, still proceed from the transformations of consciousness. How could it be that things, images arise from emptiness? As a gatha in the *Śūraṃgama-sūtra* says,

> The great awakening emerging from emptiness
> Is like a single bubble in the ocean[142]

---

[139] The five organs of eyes, ears, nose, tongue and skin together with their five objects of form, sound, odour, taste and tactile objects.

[140] Zhiyi's commentary on the *Lotus Sutra*. T1716.33.0696a14.

[141] The three contemplations 三觀 *san guan* are, contemplation of emptiness 空觀, which negates mistaken notions of conventional reality; contemplation of the nominal (or relative) 假觀; contemplation of the middle 中觀, which harmonises the above two viewpoints but is not attached to any of them.

[142] 首楞嚴義疏注經 *Shoulengyan yishu zhu jing,* 'An Annotated Commentary on the

Therefore a commentary on the *Huayan Jing* says, 'Emptiness and existence are two dharmas'[143] – both are referred to as the true principle, so existence and emptiness are both of the nature of emptiness. The sub-commentary says,

> As for emptiness and existence being referred to as the true principle, this emptiness is the external emptiness [of objects]. If the emptiness of principle confronts external emptiness, then external emptiness is **[426a]** free of/apart from (離法) dharmas; it is the emptiness of cessation/elimination (斷滅). The emptiness of principle then is called true emptiness. As with external emptiness, so also the manifestation of consciousness; again, by means of coming up against forms, the cessation of forms (滅色) is then evident – so that this [too] is the elimination of emptiness (斷空). From conditions there is no inherent existence – precisely the emptiness of nature. Therefore, within the eighteen emptinesses[144] clarity is great, referred to as the emptiness of the ten directions, which is complete voidness of the ten directions, also the emptiness of nature.[145]

Therefore a thousand sages are entrusted with the transmission, but it is difficult to encounter the opportune conditions. When faced with superior root faculties it is clearly verifiable, as a poem by Hanshan relates, [146]

Meaning of the *Śūraṃgama-sūtra*' (n. d.) (*Śūraṃgama-sūtra* was translated by Pramiti 般刺蜜帝 705CE). T1799.39.0872a03.

[143] Chengguan's commentary. T1735.35.0802a05.

[144] 十八空 eighteen forms of *śūnyatā*, as taught in the *Mahāprajñāpāramitā-Sūtra* (摩訶般若波羅蜜經 T 223): internal emptiness 內空, external emptiness 外空, internal/external emptiness 內外空, empty emptiness 空空, great emptiness 大空, ultimate emptiness 第一義空, conditioned emptiness 有爲空, unconditioned emptiness 無爲空, final emptiness 畢竟空, beginningless emptiness 無始空, dispersed emptiness 散空, emptiness of nature 性空, emptiness of self-marks 自相空, emptiness of all dharmas, 諸法空, emptiness of non-attainability 不可得空, emptiness of nonexistence 無法空, emptiness of existence 有法空, emptiness of existence and nonexistence 無法有法空.

[145] Chengguan's sub-commentary.T1736.36.0152b24.

[146] For Hanshan's poem see *The Poetry of Hanshan (Cold Mountain), Shide, and Fenggan,* Translated by Paul Rouzer. Master Yanshou makes changes to some of the lines of Hanshan's poem.

From ancient times, many sages 自古多少聖
Took pains to exhort by way of language 語路苦叮嚀
People's root natures are not equal 人根性不等
High or low, they are sharp or dull 高下有利鈍
The true Buddha is not willingly acknowledged 真佛不肯信
Focussing on achievement is to suffer in vain 置功抂147受困
Not as good as a purified lucid consciousness 不如心淨明
This is already the seal of the Dharma King 便是心王印

Hanshan's verse
自古多少聖
叮嚀教自信
人根性不等
高下有利鈍
真佛不肯認
置功枉受困
不知清淨心
便是法王印

Yanshou's verse
自古多少聖
語路苦叮嚀
人根性不等
高下有利鈍
真佛不肯**信**
置功**抂**受困
不如心淨明
便是**心王印**

A former worthy said that the desire to know the essentials of the Dharma – that consciousness is the root origin of the twelve divisions of the Buddhist canon[148] – is to enter the essential gate of the path. As for this consciousness-gate and the three periods (past, present and future) of Buddhas and patriarchs, only this one matter is real. The other two are really not true, for there is only the Dharma of the one vehicle, neither two nor three. Concerning the Dharma of the one vehicle, the one consciousness is it, so just guard the one consciousness, verily consciousness's gate to thusness. [Although] there is nothing lacking in any dharma, no conditioned dharmas (法行) come from consciousness; only consciousness itself knows [its reality]. Furthermore, it is consciousness without any separation; consciousness without form, without a root, non-abid-

---

[147] 抂＝枉.

[148] *Sūtra*, (*geya*) verses, *gāthā* (verse part of a discourse), *nidāna* (historical narratives), *itivṛttaka* (activities of Buddha or his disciples in past lives), *jātaka* (Buddha's past life stories), *adbhuta-dharma* (Buddha's miraculous acts), *avadāna* (legends), *upadeśa* (didactic lessons), *udāna* (teachings offered by the Buddha without prompting), *vaipulya* (expanded teachings), *vyākaraṇa* (guarantees of future attainment).

ing, neither coming to be nor ceasing to be; nor is there an awakening to be attained by the practice of meditative insight. Were there such a practice as analytical contemplation, then it would be sensation, perception, volition and consciousness,[149] all these are functions of bodily processes (功用), not the [function of the] original consciousness.

All the patriarchs simply transmit by means of consciousness to consciousness[150] – those who arrive are approved. Neither is there another Dharma. As in the *Huayan Sūtra*, Mañjuśri bodhisattva taught five hundred youths to arouse the conscious aspiration to awaken (發菩提心). Only one, Sudhana, came to the original source of consciousness. Travelling to one hundred and ten cities, he asked about the myriad practices [leading to awakening]. The samadhi-gates he studied were all illusory and insubstantial, so it is known that all which arises from consciousness is the same as illusory transformations. Just awaken directly to the true consciousness, a self-existent reality (自然真實). As the *Essentials of the Discourse on Only Consciousness* says,

To rely on objects, teachings, principle, practice and results, these five within [the context of] 'Only [projections of] Consciousness' (唯識) is the purpose of this treatise. It focuses exclusively on objects as being only [projections of] consciousness, freeing consciousness from grasping objects outside because no objects are apart from consciousness – [this] is the meaning […] It only discusses the teaching of 'Only Consciousness' as originally taught in the *Chenglun*[151] and explains what is discussed – this is the purpose. It focuses exclusively on the principle of 'Only Consciousness' to establish the original teaching of principle as discussed, to differentiate 'Only Consciousness' into nature (noumenal) and characteristics (性相) is the meaning. Focusing on 'Only Consciousness' as application, it clarifies the five stages of cultivating the practice of the Yogācāra path, this is the purpose;[152] by focusing only on the fruit of 'Only Consciousness' it

---

[149] 受想行識 The four mental aggregates—*vedanā, saṃjñā, saṃskāra, vijñāna*.

[150] Often translated as 'heart to heart' or 'mind to mind' transmission.

[151] 成唯識論 T1585.

[152] 唯識修道五位 *weishi xiudao wuwei*, the five stages of cultivating the Yogacara path: the stage of preparation (資糧位), the stage of application (加行位), the stage of proficiency (通達位), the stage of practice (修習位) and the stage of completion (究竟位).

searches the great fruit of the happy liberation body (解脱身) – therefore the great sage Buddha is called the Dharma.[153]

So far, in order to now explain this discussion, only the teaching as principle is taken up; it says that to rely on the teaching of principle, it becomes that [noumenal] nature and characteristics – therefore the nature (noumenal) and characteristics assimilate all entirely. Everything, if taken up in terms of principle, is the superior, it is known as the principle of [**426b**] 'Only Consciousness' (唯識之理), the authentic teaching (正宗) of the accomplished Buddhas. Only through principle is it all-inclusive, for there is no dharma that is not [included] and therefore it is called the 'Only Consciousness' of all dharmas. It explicates the authentic meaning of the Ancestral Mirror teachings (宗鏡), the thorough-going original intention of the Buddhas and patriarchs. Catering only for the one capacity [for awakening] (逗一機), through only one Dharma – there is, again, no other aim. Therefore the *Fahua Jing* says,

> In the Buddha lands of the ten directions there is only the Dharma of the single vehicle.[154]

The *Mahāparanirvāṇa-Sūtra* says,

> As to the lion's roar, it proclaims the certitude that all living beings are fully endowed with the Buddha-nature.

It also says,

> These living beings are also fully endowed with consciousness and all those in possession of consciousness will attain supreme and perfect enlightenment.[155]

426b07

Question: The three realms are only consciousness (唯心), the myriad dharmas

---

[153] 唯識樞要 *weishi shu yao*, 'Essentials of the Discourse on Theory of Only Consciousness [in the Palm of the Hand]' (成唯識論掌中樞要) by Kuiji 窺基 (632–682 CE). T1831.43.0610a05.

[154] T1716.33.0797c10.

[155] T0375.12.0767a28 and 0769a20.

Only Consciousness (唯識); should there be a source teaching (宗) on *thusness* established separately from these all-embracing dharmas?

426b08

Answer: Thusness is of the nature of consciousness. Since consciousness embraces the myriad dharmas, it is of the nature of the equality of all dharmas, existent or non-existent. Thus a sutra says, 'Not one dharma has ever existed'[156] yet [these dharmas] come forth from the nature of Dharma. Sima Biao said, 'Nature: it is the root of the human being.' Cai Yong said, 'Nature: it is the root of consciousness.'[157] Thus spoke the masters of old.

In treatises discussing 'Only Consciousness' the ten supporting [Yogacara treatises][158] are the loftiest branches of the Dharma banner. What dharmas then would not be included? Which teaching not established? Just by taking simplicity as the meaning,[159] so consciousness takes awakening as its meaning; apart from consciousness there is no other exclusive substance. That is, consciousness has a function beyond the obscured consciousness, thus it is named 'only'; the designation 'only' means unique (獨), embracing both nature (noumenon) and characteristics. Thusness is the nature of consciousness and relying on various (他) mentally engendered constructs (相分), [occasioned by] forms in the outside world etc., is the characteristic[s] of consciousness. Consciousness

---

[156] T1735.35.0514c16.

[157] Master Yanshou is quoting from 肇論疏 *Zhaolun shu*, 'Commentary on the Zhao lun' by Yuankang 元康 (7th cent), T1859.45.0185a21 (肇論 by Sengzhao 僧肇; T 1858.45). 司馬彪 Sima Biao was an historian and nobleman during the Jin dynasty of China, died 306 CE; author of 續漢書 'Continued History of the Han.' Cai Yong 蔡邕 (132–192 CE) was a Chinese astronomer, calligrapher, historian, mathematician, musician, politician, and writer of the Eastern Han dynasty.

[158] The ten Yogacara treatises, the foundational work being the 瑜伽論 *Yogâcārabhūmi-śāstra*, translated into Chinese by Xuanzang 玄奘 (646–648). Authorship is attributed to Maitreya 彌勒, (Tibetan tradition to Asaṅga 無著). The others are: *Treatise on the Hundred Dharmas* 百法論; *Treatise on the Five Aggregates* 五蘊論; *Treatise of Acclamation of the Noble Teaching* 顯揚論; *Mahāyānasaṃgraha* 攝大乘論; *Exegesis on the Collection of Mahāyāna Abhidharma* 雜集論; *Madhyânta-vibhāga* 辨中邊論; *Viṃśatikā-śāstra* 二十唯識論; *Triṃśikā* 三十唯識論; *Sūtrâlaṃkāra-śāstra* 大莊嚴論; *Fenbie yuqie lun* 分別瑜伽論. Muller/Dan Lusthaus, DDB.

[159] 識簡心空 Kuiji. T1830.43.0229b26.

61

is that which takes consciousness as the master, nothing is therefore separate from consciousness and collectively this is called 'Only Consciousness'.[160]

426b17

Another question: The three realms contain contaminated outflows of dharmas, due to people being fettered by the bonds of desire in the three realms, hence the name three realms. But their unconditioned and uncontaminated dharmas are not tethered by desires for the three realms; that is, it is not called the Dharma of the three realms. Why then do sutras solely declare that the three realms are only consciousness, which really does not include (unite with 不攝) such as the unconditioned and uncontaminated dharmas? This is surely not [the doctrine of] 'Only Consciousness', for it only talks of three realms?

426b21

Answer: The three realms that are governed by afflicted, confused dharmas are nevertheless called 'Only Consciousness' (唯識). The unconditioned and uncontaminated Dharma is [noumenal] nature able to govern, for its essence is not confused; it is not said to be self-contained (自成), therefore it is simply said that the three realms are only consciousness (唯心). Furthermore,

> The general term in all schools has it that existence and non-existence, defiled and pure dharmas are all rooted in consciousness. As the Sarvastivāda School and others say,[161] it is due to the unconditioned [Dharma] of consciousness that it manifests and due to the conditioned [dharmas] of consciousness that they arise. Defiled and pure dharmas arise from consciousness since potent conditions are strong, so it is said that consciousness is the root.[162]

---

[160] 識性識相皆不離心 心所心王以識爲主. T1830.43.0229b25.

[161] 薩婆多 (說一切有部) Sarvāstivāda School, one of the major branches of Indian Abhidharma Buddhism, which developed some 200 years after Śākyamuni's death. They denied the existence of a unitary self 我, but believed in the inherent existence of dharmas 法 (phenomena). Its doctrines are defined in the *Abhidharmakośa-bhāṣya*.

[162] T1831.43.0637a23.

Question: How many entrances to meritorious power can evoke faith in what is seen and heard by establishing consciousness as the teaching?

Answer: The intrinsic nature (自體) of true consciousness is not something to be explained in words. It is as deep as boundless space, as lustrous as a round and bright pure mirror. Praise and blame do not come up to it. The [interpretation of its] principle (義理) is difficult to penetrate, since the two poles of meritorious power and affliction are [**426c**] absolutely irrelevant (絕對待). Now, according to former worthies, concerning consciousness's distinguishing of characteristics, these are, briefly, of five interpretations: the first characteristic is detachment from the attribute of discrimination regarding what is discerned (取); second is liberated from a subjective grasping at distinctions apprehended; third, that the all-pervasive three realms are without any inequality; the fourth, that there is nowhere that the equality of the realm of emptiness (śūnyatā) does not reach to; the fifth interpretation, that [consciousness] does not fall into either poles of existence or non-existence, sameness or difference. These [five characteristics] transcend the sphere of mental functions (心行處) and are beyond the way of words.

Furthermore,

This is the non-abidingness of consciousness, negating the two truths [of the absolute and relative], so that there is no difference between leaving the relative and entering the real/absolute – and since there is no difference between leaving [the one] and entering [the other], it is neither in emptiness nor in existence. Therefore a sutra says that consciousness is not a place, is not located anywhere as a state. There is only one (universal) consciousness and the essence of consciousness is originally quiescent.[163]

Its hidden traces are not ultimately accessible, neither in the states of existence nor non-existence. Neither is it possible with mental constructs/knowledge (識智), nor analytical explanations, to discuss its ineffable essence. Only the

---

[163] 金剛三昧經論 *Commentary on the Geumgang sammae gyeong* (*Jingang sanmei jing*, Diamond Sutra). Exegesis by the Korean scholar-monk Wonhyo 元曉 (617–686) translated by Robert Buswell in *Cultivating Original Enlightenment*. T1730.34.0979b21.

ones who enter just know it in their consciousness. It is like grinding down ten thousand seeds in order to produce a fragrant pill; burning one mote of dust to provide multiple fragrances / energies; it is like entering the waters of the great ocean in order to bathe; scooping up a tiny drop is already scooping up a hundred rivers; to hold gravel fast, then it ultimately turns into real gold; gathering up grass, then it is nothing but wonderful medicine. The empty vessel is completely filled with the flavour of nectar – filling the room is only the perfume of the *champaka*;[164] all meanings return to the original home, as if the great void would contain all phenomena, a thousand roads vigorously entered; it is like a thousand shadows that do not obstruct a pure deep lake.

If the discussion is about the virtuous power arising from the nature of universal consciousness: it is inexhaustible and without limits. How, by the possession of a calculating consciousness, could one praise the power of non-being? To definitively take on spiritual strength has hardly ever been narrated because people entering in faith all come to direct realisation, be they worldling or sage. Human feelings and the response [of the Buddhas 感應] is not unreal (非虛); firm faith does not move. The sound of Dharma's empty emptiness is of itself calming; its clarity and sincerity can be examined; wild-fires are put to a stop by numinous rains. Would this be counterfeit spiritual cognition? As the demons of consciousness are suddenly cut off there is no reliance on other methods; acknowledging the fire, it melts away of itself, but does not eliminate the person. How to clarify this teaching? An ancient said,

> Rely on wisdom, not on mental constructs:[165] it means that mental constructs are active, discerning imaginary dusts; eyes coloured, ears hearing sounds, sunk in delusion and not realising it. The great sage (Buddha) taught that phenomena are all from consciousness; the most foolish are frozen in grasping. Dust is the external aspect of mental constructs and these days people intone (口誦) these in vain, but consciousness never forgets.[166] They soar in vain [but] do not rise, entering the fire of great difficulties

---

[164] *Magnolia champaca* is an aromatic tree with fragrant yellow flowers.

[165] One of the four Dharma reliances 法四依: rely on the Buddhist teachings not on men 依法不依人; rely on the meaning not on the words 依義不依語; rely wisdom (Skt. *prajñā*) not on mental constructs 依智不依識; rely on the complete teaching sutras not on the incomplete teachings 依了義經不依不了義經. T0374.12.0401b27.

[166] 亡 / 忘.

64

（騰空不起入火逾難）, all because the characteristics of consciousness are sealed in delusion. Later, understanding is obtained and then, in accord with consciousness, the functioning changes. How could this not be the same as a bird wheeling free through empty space? It is as necessary as a non-inflammable robe (自當如是布之火浣).[167] It is also not surprising (不足怪也) but that the collective nature of sentient beings' consciousness is not the same, causing the great sage's discourse to accord with different dispositions. Nevertheless, according to the ultimate path, there is simply one's own consciousness. Therefore the sutra says that in the three realms, above and below, the meaning of the Dharma is 'Only Consciousness.' This then is the explanation the world relies on by clarifying the luminous consciousness. It also says that thusness and the highest reality (真際), nirvana and the realm of Dharma are various types of mind-engendered entities (Skt. *manomaya-kāya*). I (Daoxuan) describe these as mental inferences (心量) – this is in accord with [**427a**] the luminous consciousness as a transmundane Dharma essence, which finally reaches ultimate reality, in the end coming to the source (原/源) by following the stream of actions and their fruition (感果), the return to the definitive meaning of the teaching.[168]

427a02

Question: How could the one consciousness be regarded as the essential doctrine within the teachings? There is broad discussion of various ways and each is set up as a doctrinal theme of a sutra.

427a03

Answer: although the various kinds of Dharma [teachings] are many, only the one consciousness is that which is written of; on the basis of the noble path countless names were set up. Likewise on account of a single fire burning, various names are generated, such as grass fire, and wood fire. Similarly when a single drop of fluid is put to use and a multiple of names are found, of soups or wines. This single gate of consciousness is likewise just so; in response to [those of] lesser faculties it is referred to as the lesser Dharma teachings. Evinc-

---

[167] 釋門歸敬儀 *Shimen guijingyi*, 'Returning to the School of Śākyamuni with Reverent Observances' by Daoxuan 道宣 (596–667). T1896.45.0860c11. (常 amended to 當 T1896.45.0860c28 – T2016.48.0426c25).

[168] Daoxuan. T1896.45.0861a14.

ing the superior level then is called the great vehicle. Although the greater and lesser differ, the true nature is not divided. Were there a determination to insist that the Buddha-utterance (Skt. *buddha-vacana*) consisted of multiple dharmas, that would be to defame the Wheel of the Dharma,[169] incurring the fault of slander, which is why a sutra says,

Consciousness is not separate from the Way, the Way is not separate from consciousness. [170]

The *Mahāparanirvāṇa-Sūtra* says,

At that time the World-honoured One praised Kāśyapa Bodhisattva, 'Excellent, quite excellent oh son of good family! Now you wish to know the secrets of the profound sutras of the bodhisattvas' great vehicle, thus putting the question. Son of good family! All the sutras are such that they all enter the truth of the Way. Good son! As I have said before, if there is faith in the Way, the path of the Way is thus; this faith being the root, it can support the Way to bodhi and so it is explained by me, without there being any mistake. Good son! The Tathāgata knows well immeasurable expedient means and wishes to transform living beings and so works to give a variety of discourses such as this on the Dharma. Good son! Take the example of a good physician who knows the various illnesses of all sentient beings. He follows their ailments and then applies the appropriate medicine. Moreover, the medicine is not restricted to one kind of decoction: [be it] a ginger decoction, or liquorice decoction or black-stone honey decoction

---

169 法輪 *falun,* the term translated as 'wheel' – *cakra,* was a kind of weapon in ancient India. Therefore, the *dharmacakra* is a weapon that is able to crush all evil. [...] Like Indra's wheel, it rolls on from man to man, place to place, age to age – the teachings of the Buddha. It is turned by the Wheel Turning Sage Kings 轉輪聖王. (Pāli *dhammacakka*). DDB.

170 佛昇忉利天爲母說法經 *Fo sheng daoli tianwei mu shuo fa jing,* 'The sutra in which Buddha ascends to the Heaven of the thirty-three [celestials] to preach the Dharma for his mother.' The thirty-three celestials live on the top of Mt. Sumeru, in the second of the six heavens of the desire realm 六欲天. Śakra 帝釋天 (Pāli: Sakka), also known as Indra, dwells in the centre with eight other gods in each of the four directions. See the eight Vasus, eleven Rudras, twelve Ādityas, and two Aśvins in *Bhagavad Gita,* Chapter ii: The Universal Form. To815.17.0789c0i.

(sugar cane from Guanzhou) or a tamarind (*Tamarindus indica*) decoction, or Nepalese [Himalayan] water (?尼婆羅水) or an Udaka (Hribera *Pavonia odorata*) concoction or prescribes iced water or hot water or grape juice or a calming pomegranate decoction. Good son! In this way a good physician knows well the various sufferings of sentient beings and the remedies, although many are not restricted to these examples.

'The Tathāgata likewise well knows the expedient means [in relation to] the one Dharma. Complying with the characteristics of all sentient beings he broadly discourses on various names and appearances so that those beings can follow what they have received and having received, engage in practice to be able to extirpate afflictions. Like those sick people following the advice of a good physician, that which is afflicting can be eradicated.

'Furthermore, oh good son, suppose there is a person who well understands the words of many amongst a great crowd. This crowd of people is overcome by a burning thirst; they give rise to a cry saying, "I want to drink some water, I want to drink water!" This person then gives them cool, clear water, each according to their need saying, "This is water," or calling it *boni, yanchi, suoliyan, poli, boye* [**427b**] or calling it nectar or cow's milk – using such innumerable names for water, he explains it to the great crowd. Good son, the Tathāgata likewise expounds on the one noble path by giving various discourses for the sake of his listeners (*śrāvakas*), from the faculty of faith and so on, to arriving at the noble eightfold path.

'Again oh good son, a goldsmith, for example, fashions all kinds of jewellery from the same gold, according to his wish; such as necklaces, bracelets, rings, hair pins, heavenly crowns and elbow bands – although so different, nevertheless they are not separate from [the same] gold. Good son, the Tathāgata likewise, by means of the single Buddhist path, teaches in various ways according to the circumstances of living beings and the discourse is for their sakes. Either the discourse is of one kind, in which case it is referred to as the single path of the Buddha, not two. But again, the discourse of two kinds is referred to as meditation and wisdom, or yet again, his discourse is of three kinds, referred to as insight, wisdom and knowledge; again, four kinds of discourse is referred to as the path of seeing, the path of practice, the path of nothing further to learn and the path of a Buddha. Discoursing on up to twenty paths refers to the Ten Powers,[171]

---

[171] Distinguishing right and wrong; knowing what is right or wrong in every condition 處

the Four Fearlessnesses,[172] great kindness, great compassion, the samadhi of remembering the Buddha and the three correct bases of mindfulness. Good son, this path is one but in days gone by the Tathāgata expounded the Dharma in various ways for the sake of living beings.

'Once more, oh good son, the example is of a fire; because of what is burnt it gets a variety of names, called a wood fire, a grass fire, rice-bran fire, chaff fire, cow or horse dung fire. Good son, likewise the Buddha-way is one, not two, but for the sake of living beings, various ways are differentiated.

'Furthermore oh good son, the example of unified consciousness is spoken of as having six [aspects]. If it reaches the eye then it is called eye-consciousness, all the way up to the thought consciousness (Skt. *manovijñāna*). Oh good son, the Way is like this too – it is one, not two, but for the sake of transforming all living beings the Tathāgata presents various differentiations.

'Furthermore oh good son, the example is of form / colour – what is seen by the eye is called form; what the ear hears is called sound; what the nose smells is called fragrance; what the tongue tastes is called taste; what the body feels is called touch. Good son, the Way is like this, it is one, not two. The Tathāgata, for the sake of wishing to transform living beings, presents various differentiations. Good son, that is the meaning for the Noble Eightfold Path being called the Noble Truth of the Way. Good son, these Four Noble Truths are expounded sequentially by all the World-honoured Bud-

---

非處智力; knowing one's own karma, as well as knowing the karma of every being, past, present, and future 自業智力; or knowing karmic ripening 業異熟智力; knowledge of all forms of meditation; knowing all stages of *dhyāna* liberation, and samādhi 靜慮解脫等持等至智力; knowledge of the relative capacities of sentient beings 根勝劣智力 (or 根上下智力); knowledge of what sentient beings have devoted interest in; the desires, or moral direction of every being 種種勝解智力; knowledge of the varieties of causal factors (seeds 種子) 種種界智力; knowledge of the gamut of courses and paths pursued by sentient beings 遍趣行智力; knowledge of remembrance of past lives □住隨念智力; knowledge of where people will die and be reborn 死生智力; knowledge of the methods of destroying all contamination 漏盡智力.

[172] 正等覺無畏, fearlessness in asserting that he has attained perfect enlightenment; 漏永盡無畏, fearlessness in asserting that he has destroyed all contamination; 說障法無畏, fearlessness in showing people those elements which hinder the realisation of the Dharma, and 說出道無畏, fearlessness in expounding the method of liberation.

68

dhas. Due to these causes and conditions, innumerable sentient beings are able to cross the sea of birth and death.'[173]

It is also said,

> If there is talk of ten kinds of wholesome behaviours and ten kinds of unwholesome behaviours, of what can be done and what cannot be done, of wholesome paths and unwholesome paths, of white dharmas and black dharmas, then it is ordinary folk speaking in two's. Wise ones understand this nature as not-two. The nature of non-duality is precisely the real nature.[174]

The *Dhāraṇī-sūtra* says,

> A multitude of dharmas does not exist and this is called the one-word Dharma-gate.[175]

Another sutra reports the Buddha as saying that of the Dharma expounded by all the Buddhas of the three realms [or time], [**427c**] 'I, in the present forty-nine years, have not added a single word.'[176] Know therefore, that this is the gate of the one consciousness, capable of accomplishing the ultimate path. If someone of superior faculties enters directly, then another entrance will never be established. For those of middling or lower [faculties] who have yet to enter, there is then the expedient division into various paths, to which the Buddhas and patriarchs collectively pointed. The noble ones return unseen; although of different names, they are of the same essence; conditioned by circumstances yet harmonious in essence – wisdom (*prajñā*) only pronounces it as not-two.

The *Lotus* [sutra] only expounds the one vehicle; the *Vimalakirti*, nothing other than the sanctuary of the Way; the *Nirvana* [sutras] all return to the secret treasury of the profound wisdom; *Tiantai* focuses endeavour on the

---

[173] To375.12.0683b10.

[174] To375.12.0651c06.

[175] 金剛場陀羅尼經 *Jingangchang tuoluoni jing*, 'Dhāraṇī of the Adamantine Place', translation by Jñānagupta 闍那崛多 (523–600/605?). T1345.21.0856a04.

[176] No exact match.

Three Contemplations;[177] *Jiangxi* (Mazu) takes the essence as the whole truth, for Mazu then, the Buddha is consciousness; Heze directly points to knowledge by insight.[178]

Furthermore, the teachings are expounded in two ways – the first explanation is explicit, the second, esoteric. As for the explicit teachings, this applies to the *Laṅkāvatāra-Sūtra*, the *Densely Adorned Sutra* [179] and others, as well as treatises such as *The Arising of Faith* and *Only Consciousness*. As for the esoteric teachings, each one is based on a doctrinal theme from the sutras (經宗), to which different names are applied, just as the *Vimalakirti* takes 'the inconceivable' as its teaching, the *Diamond Sutra* 'non-abiding,' the *Huayan* 'the Dharma-realm of reality' and as the *Nirvāṇa-Sūtra* takes 'the Buddha-nature' as its teaching.

Any of a thousand roads can be set up, as all are distinct meanings of the one consciousness. How so? It is because the true consciousness's ineffable essence does not abide in existence or non-existence, cannot be known by wise knowledge, is not accessible by words, is not of the realm of feelings or calculation. Therefore it is referred to as the inconceivable.

Essence, emptiness and phenomena are quiescent, free of expectations (絕 待). Numinous penetration of the mundane realm of phenomena is the unborn transcending the three realms of time, cutting off [all] traces. Therefore it is called non-abiding.

Penetrating the three realms, stretching across the ten directions without limit, the extent of its boundaries is unreachable. Therefore, it is referred to as the Dharma-realm, the root of the ten thousand things, the primordial cause of all beings. In the worldly it does not decrease, in the state of nobility there is no increase; numinous awareness is clear, ever true to its essence. Therefore it is called the Buddha-nature, or sometimes even called the ineffable nature of

---

[177] The view of emptiness, of dependent arising and the middle view.

[178] Heze Shenhui 荷澤神會 (668–760). Chan monk, disciple of Huineng 慧能, considered to be the founder of the Heze 荷澤 school of Chinese Chan, being a primary representative of the southern 'sudden' tradition.

[179] 大乘密嚴經 *Dasheng miyan jing, Ghana-vyūha*, 'Great Vehicle Sutra of [the Pure Land], Densely Adorned' translated twice into Chinese, the first time by Divākara 地 婆訶羅 (676–688) (T 681) and the second time by Amoghavajra 不空金剛 (705–774). (T 682). Its doctrines resemble those of the *Laṅkâvatāra-Sūtra* 楞伽經.

the numinous terrace, the precious treasury of spiritual pearls – all are the one consciousness, called differently according to conditions. A sutra says,

> The hundreds of thousands of names of the three incalculably long aeons are all different appellations of the Tathāgata.[180]

Merely due to not knowing the expedient means of all the Buddhas, tricked by names, attached to phenomenal appearances, to accord with [this kind of] understanding becomes error. Only by penetrating this source (宗) is one suddenly awoken to the empty quiescence – what names or characteristics would there be to reveal?

It is like the Dragon King's single flavour of rain, following the wholesome and unwholesome karma of men and devas, the rain falls differently, each one seeing it otherwise. The *Huayan Sūtra* says,

> It is like the Ocean Dragon King[181] wishing to manifest as a dragon king, his great unimpeded power is for the benefit of all sentient beings, causing all joy. He descends from the [formless] heaven of the four quarters to the heavenly realms where [the devas] partake freely of the pleasures created by [karma in] other heavens.[182] And on earth, in all places, the rain falls indifferently – called raining clear cool water amidst the great ocean, called: uninterrupted. In the sixth heaven of desire a variety of music, such as of flutes, rain down and all kinds of music are called exquisitely beautiful. In the fifth heaven of desire[183] it rains down with great [**428a**] *maṇi* treasures, called emitting magnificent radiance. In the fourth heaven of desire,[184] the *Tuṣita* heaven, the rain is of great ornaments, called pendant topknots. In the heaven of Yama[185] it rains wonderful flowers, called all kinds of adorn-

---

[180] 楞伽阿跋多羅寶經 *Lengqie abaduoluo Baojing*, 'The Precious sutra of *Laṅkâvatāra*', Guṇabhadra's 求那跋陀羅 (394–468) partial translation. T0670.16.0506b05.

[181] One of eight great dragon kings.

[182] The sixth of the six heavens of desire, the last of the six devalokas, the abode of Mahêśvara (i. e. Śiva), and of Māra. The denizens of this heaven enjoy all the felicities derived from the karma of the other five levels of the desire realms.

[183] 化樂天 The fifth heaven of desire, where every joy is obtainable.

[184] 兜率天 The fourth heaven of desire, where future Buddhas await birth on earth.

[185] 夜摩天 The third heaven of Yama, lord of the underworld, where one day equals two hundred earth years.

ments. In the heaven of the thirty-three[186] wonderful perfumes rain down, called joy. In the heaven of the Four Celestial Quarters[187] it rains divine jewelled garments, called coverings. In the palace of the Dragon King it rains genuine red pearls, called radiance springing forth. In the palace of the Asuras[188] it rains all kinds of armaments, called forcing enemies into submission. In the Uttarakuru in the North[189] all kinds of flowers rain down, called blooming flowers. The other three continents are also like this. Nevertheless, each accords with its own place, for what rains down is not the same. Although those consciousnesses of the Dragon Kings are equal, with no difference between them, it is because the good roots of living beings differ that there is difference in rains.[190]

This is why the Dragon Kings' rain is of a single taste; the response of all the Devas complies with appropriate situations, which are not the same. It is like the Dharma-gate of the one (universal) consciousness of all the Buddhas, there are distinctions according to when living beings see it.

End of Fascicle Two

---

[186] *Trāyastriṃśa* Heaven of the celestials, the second heaven of desire; the denizens live for one thousand years, one day being equivalent to one hundred years.

[187] 四天王 guardians of the four quarters of the universe.

[188] 阿脩羅 demigods consumed by sensuous existence, endlessly engaged in wars against the gods.

[189] 北欝單越 Uttarakuru, the northernmost of the four continents 四洲 around Meru 須彌, square in shape, inhabited by square-faced people. Its inhabitants are about 60 feet tall, and have a lifespan of 1,000 years, with food being produced without human effort. Emotional experiences and all material things are wonderful there. DDB.

[190] T0279.10.0269b24.

Records from the Ancestral Mirror

Fascicle Three

Now the teachings clarify the myriad dharmas. The ultimate principle is empty, ineffable. No explanations of existence or non-existence can cut through the nature of self and other, but if there is no intrinsic essence to any dharmas, how can one establish a source teaching (宗)?

Answer: If a source teaching (宗) is not established, how could a practice turn towards the [Buddhist] path? Given the discussions of the existence or non-existence of self and other, these are all distinctions of the cognitive faculties of living beings, [yet] this is the entrance to the cure. Interconnectedness is the intrinsic nature of the Dharma-body and the true aspect of the middle way is the principle of consciousness (理心) – would that be the same as illusory existence? Following neither illusions nor non-existence, the *Laṅkāvatāra-Sūtra* has the Buddha saying,

> Great wisdom, for example, is not of the nature of an ox or a horse. Truly the nature of an ox or a horse is neither existent nor non-existent, yet they are not without distinctive characteristics.[191]

An old commentator says,

> Nothing can be attributed to the body of a horse, or the existence or non-existence of the nature of an ox; however, it is not that the horse does not have an intrinsic nature (自體).[192]

---

[191] T0670.16.0505c05.

[192] Source unclear; (not T1791.39.0484a10. 注大乘入楞伽經 composed by 'Shamen' Baochen 寶臣 of the Song dynasty?).

By analogy, whether the nature of the aggregates, elements and bases[193] exist or do not exist cannot be attributed to the Dharma-body. However, it is not so that the intrinsic attribute (自相) of the Dharma-body does not exist. This principle of the emptiness of dharmas is beyond existence and non-existence, which is precisely the nature of the Dharma-body. Nevertheless, there is an impulse towards a direction. The true reality behind wisdom is that there is no attainment, no return, no deluded thinking arising and ceasing; quite simply these [already] exist so there is no need to [**428b**] search for thusness, rules or winding ways: without these it (the true reality) is naturally self-sufficient. The subtle purport shimmers bright, so quiescence is the return home, tranquil and continuous. Suddenly the dichotomy of perceiver and perceived (能所)[194] is transcended. Being neither existent nor non-existent, it can be called a return to thusness (真歸), no less than (矣) the ability to penetrate the ultimate path.

428b03

Question: By taking consciousness as the teaching, how is the characteristic of the teaching completely understood?

428b04

Answer: The internal realisation of one's own consciousness is the first principle – to abide in the stage of self-realisation and enter the gate of sagely wisdom. By means of this accordance with true principle (相應) it is called complete penetration of the teaching. This is the time of practice, not the time of explanations (解). Since explanations become practice, practice completes the severance of explanations – then it is called the path of discourse cut off and the state of mental operations (心行處) ceases, as the *Laṅkâvatāra-Sūtra* relates,

> The Buddha told Mahāmati,[195] 'Those who penetrate the teaching are called individually attained to the characteristics of the superior Way; they are far, far removed from the deluded notions of words and phrases and hasten to the stage of the intrinsic attributes of the untainted realm of self-realisation;

---

[193] The five aggregates 五陰, twelve sense bases 十二入, and eighteen elements of cognition 十八界 (Skt. *skandha-dhātu-āyatana, skandhâyatana-dhātu*).

[194] 能所 as 體用 see DDB under these terms.

[195] Mahāmati (大慧/摩訶摩底/馬曷麻諦/大意菩薩), the interlocutor bodhisattva of the *Laṅkâvatāra-Sūtra* and other texts.

74

they are far, far removed from all vacuous or deceptive feelings or perceptions and subdue all the demons of the heterodox ways. Self-realised, their path forward shines brightly. This is called the oneness of penetrating the teachings (宗通相).'[196]

Therefore an awakened consciousness becomes a patriarch; the sages of old transmit one to another, which is why great master Bodhidharma said,

> Clarify the Buddha-heart school (consciousness) teachings. Awakening is without an inch of a discrepancy; practice and liberation is in accordance with the true principle (相應), so he is called a patriarch.[197]

And a gatha says,

> Look neither on evil, giving rise to resentment
> Nor observe the good by diligently forcing it
> Discard neither the foolish to be intimate with the worthy
> Nor abandon confusion to come to enlightenment
>
> Come to the Great Way: it is beyond measure
> Penetrate the Buddha-heart (consciousness): cross to the other
> shore
> For sages and worldlings the route is different
> Going beyond, it is called being a patriarch[198]

428b16

Question: Awakening to the path clarifies the teaching, like a person drinking

---

[196] T0670.16.0499b29.

[197] 小室六門 *Xiaoshi liumen,* 'Xiaoshi's Six Gates' supposedly by Bodhidharma. It is a Japanese compilation, earliest extant edition Tokugawa era, 1647. The individual treatises of which it is composed, however, were written in China during the Tang 唐代 (618–907). (Erez Joskovich, DDB). T2009.48.0370a25. (Yanshou, 寸無差悟, T2009, 等無差誤).

[198] 雙峰山曹侯溪寶林傳 *Shuang feng shan cao houxi Baolinzhuan,* 'Biographies from Baolin Temple, Mnt. Shuangfeng, Caohouxi' a ten-fascicle (incomplete) collection of biographies of Chan masters at Baolinsi 寶林寺 by Zhiju 智炬 composed in 801CE. B14.0081.0138a03.

water knows intimately whether it is hot or cold: but say, how does this explain its defining activity?

428b17

Answer: As stated previously, the expedient means of all the Buddhas are not confined to present time. Deep compassion is spread covertly; they do not abandon anyone to loneliness. To those who have already attained no words at all are addressed. It is only that there are questions due to doubt that questions are answered.

This is what the original master (Buddha) said at the head of the assembly in Lanka for all the great bodhisattvas of the ten directions coming in search of the Dharma. This is a detailed explanation of these two penetrations. The first [penetration] is realisation itself (宗通); the second is a full exposition. Realisation itself is for the bodhisattvas; full expositions are for those of childlike simplicity.

The Buddhas and patriarchs see fit to bow down to beginners of childlike simplicity in order to impart a little indication – [yet] this contains a full exposition. [Beginners of childlike simplicity] merely look for the Dharma by following others; understanding arises in accordance with the exposition. Fearing to grasp that expedient means are real, there is confusion concerning realisation itself. This is the meaning of the penetrations being divided into two kinds.

As for realisation itself, it is referred to as the characteristic conditioned by individually realised superb advancement, far removed from the deluded notions of words and phrases. 'Self-realised, their path forward shines brightly.'[199] If they personally reach the stage of realisation, when the light is emitted, then it can be said that it is like a person drinking water who knows intimately whether it is warm or cold. It is like a group of blind people whose eyes have been opened, clearly illuminating the objective world. Examining forms in their real aspect, ultimately untouched by an end-state, they see the true colour of the milk.[200] Would there be chatter about its snowy swan-whiteness?[201] This is right in front of the eyes; were it necessary to indicate it with further explanations, then there would not come a time to be [428c] known by the name of great

---

[199] T0670.16.0499c02.

[200] The teaching (milk) in its five forms (colours) illustrates the Tiantai five periods of the Buddha's teaching 五時教 DCBT: 248.

[201] *Gu xue* 鵠雪.

76

Dharma teachers. Persons really seeing the moon do not after all, contemplate the finger [pointing at it]. Those who have personally come home have naturally put the process of questioning to rest. Only realisation accords with the true principle and it does not wait on explanations nor does it finally hold on to the pointing finger as being the moon; but the moon is not seen as being apart from the finger either. As the *Mahāparanirvāṇa-Sūtra* says,

Take for example a king; he tells his chief minister, 'Bring ye an elephant to show those who are blind.' At that time the minister, having received the king's command, gathered together a group of the blind to show them the elephant. Then the blind people each touched the elephant with their hands. The minister returned to the king and told him, 'Your servant has finished showing them [the elephant].' It was then that the king summoned the blind [into His presence] and asked each of them, 'Did you see the elephant?' Each of the blind replied, 'I have seen the elephant.' The king said, 'What kind of an elephant is it?' The one who had touched its tusk then said, 'The form of the elephant is like the root of a white radish;'[202] the one who had touched its ear said, 'An elephant is [shaped] like a flat wicker tray;' the one who had touched its head said, 'An elephant is [shaped] like a stone;' the one who had touched its nose said, 'An elephant is [shaped] like a small mallet;' another who had touched its foot said, 'An elephant is [shaped] like a wooden mortar;' another who had touched its back said, 'An elephant is [shaped] like a frame;' another who had touched its belly said, 'An elephant is [shaped] like a water pot;' another who had touched its tail said, 'An elephant is [shaped] like a rope.'

Oh son of good family! Just as those blind ones could not describe the body of an elephant, neither were they without an explanation. Though none of these various characteristics (radish, wicker basket, stone etc.) were of an elephant, still, apart from these, [to them] there was no other [kind of] elephant.

Good son! The king is a metaphor for the Tathāgata, Worthy [of Offerings], Perfectly Omniscient;[203] the minister is a metaphor for the *Great Nirvāṇa-Sūtra*, equally [applicable] everywhere; the elephant, a metaphor

---

[202] *Raphanus caudatus,* green / white long edible radish, shaped like a big carrot, of high medicinal value, long cultivated in Asia.

[203] A combination of three of the ten epithets 十號 of the Buddha.

for the Buddha-nature; the blind, a metaphor for all nescient beings. After hearing the Buddha's discourse, all these living beings may make this pronouncement, 'Form is the Buddha-nature.' Why? Although forms perish, it is an orderly continuum, which is why it attains the unchanging form of the unexcelled Tathāgata, the Tathāgata of the thirty-two marks. As to the form of the Tathāgata, because it is ever continuous, the form is therefore called the Buddha-nature.

Take as an example pure gold; although its material can be changed, its colour remains ever the same. At times it can be fashioned into a bracelet, fashioned into a plate, yet its golden colour never undergoes a change. The Buddha-nature of sentient beings too is just so – although its substance is not permanent yet its 'colour' is unchanging. On this account it is said that form (colour) is the Buddha-nature. It is even said that sensation, conception, volition and consciousness[204] are Buddha-nature.

Again, it is said that apart from the aggregates (skandhas) there exists an 'I'; 'I' as this Buddha-nature is like those blind people each describing an elephant: although not coming to the real [elephant]. It was not that they did not describe an elephant. Those who describe the Buddha-nature are also like this. Actually, it is not that the six things are apart from the six things. Oh good son, that is why I say that the Buddha-nature of living beings is not form, yet not apart from form; there is not even an 'I', yet there is no separation from an 'I'.

Good son! There are many heterodox paths. Although there is discussion of the existence of an 'I', yet in truth there is no 'I'. The 'I' of living beings is just the five skandhas. Apart from the five skandhas there really is no other 'I'.

Good son, take for example stems, leaves, tendrils and flower-heads – combined they make a lotus flower. [429a] Apart from this there is no other [lotus] flower. Again the Buddha said, Good son! There are those on heterodox paths; their foolishness is like that of little children, without the wisdom of expedient means. They cannot fully understand permanence or impermanence, painful or pleasant, purity or impurity, 'I' or 'no-I', a life span or no life span, living beings or non-living beings, real or unreal, existence or non-existence. Taking a small part of the Buddha's teaching,

---

[204] The four mental aggregates – *vedanā, saṃjñā, saṃskāra, vijñāna.*

78

they falsely impute an existence, permanence, happiness, 'I' and purity yet without truly knowing permanence, happiness, 'I' and purity.

It is like being born blind and not knowing the colour of milk, then asking another, 'What is the colour of milk?' The other answers, 'It is white in colour, like a shell.' Again the blind person asks, 'About the colour of milk, is it like that of a hard shell?'[205] 'No, it isn't,' comes the answer. Again a question, 'What does the colour of a shell look like?' 'It resembles rice or millet.' Again the blind one asks, 'The colour of milk is soft and gentle, is it like rice and millet? Again, rice and millet, what is it like?' Reply, 'It is similar to rain and snow.' The blind one says once more, 'Is it that rice and millet are as cold as snow? Again, what is snow like?' Answer, 'It resembles a yellow-billed swan.'

This person, born blind, although hearing these four examples, cannot, in the end, know the real colour of milk. Those on a heterodox path are also like this, unable, ultimately, to know permanence, happiness, 'I' and purity. Good son! Due to this meaning, in our Buddha-dharma there exists the real truth, not in the heterodox paths.[206]

As for the real truth, it is the Ancestral Mirror teachings (宗鏡) that return one home. Having not yet heard of the time of awakening, those who do not trust in liberation as it has been expounded in the dharma of self-cultivation all become subdued by the gates of birth and death and do not enter the ultimate Way of the Unborn. As the sutra on the maiden An Tizhe says,

At this time Mañjuśri also asked [An Tizhe], 'Is it not the case that a clear knowledge of arising yet gives no rise to characteristics; is there not a remainder of that which has arisen?' [An Tizhe] answers, 'Yes, although there is a natural clear seeing, its strength is not yet complete, so that which remains arisen exists.' [Mañjuśri] again asks, 'Could it not be that without knowledge and not aware of the nature of arising there is ultimately no conditioned arising of something which remains?' 'Not so!' came the answer, 'Why? If the nature of arising is not seen into, even through discipline, a state of peace is hardly attained and the characteristics of this restlessness

---

[205] *Ge ang* 貝鞞 shell-hard, strong, firm (T48.2016.0429a07). T0374.12.0447a01 = 貝聲.

[206] 大般涅槃經 *Da banniepan jing, Mahāparinirvāṇa-Sūtra,* 'Sutra of the Great Decease' translated by Dharmakṣema 曇無讖 (385–433). T0374.12.0556a09/0556b21/0446c24.

will always [have to] be correctly disciplined (*or* at odds with the cure 對
治). If those, although they are not in a peaceful state, are capable of insight
into the characteristics of arising, then the peaceful characteristics will always appear [to them]. If those of lesser knowledge, although having all
kinds of superior discussions, discourse on deep canonical treatises, still
it is consciousness of birth and death, explaining those true characteristics
and esoteric words as the blind discuss colour. Relying on the words of others, they talk of blue, yellow, red, white and black but cannot see the true
characteristics of colour for themselves. Now those who are unable to see
any dharmas are also like this. They are only present to there being birth
as birth, death as death and having something to say, then go to others with
"There is really no meaning to birth and death?" [**429b**] Those attached
to whether there is permanence or impermanence are also like this. Ap-
propriating the knowledge of the great attainment of emptiness they also
do not come to emptiness themselves and so ask, "Is there a meaning to
emptiness?"'[207]

Therefore, knowledge able to completely penetrate the nature of the birthlessness of the myriad dharmas, this is attaining to the Way. As the
Mahāprajñāpāramitā-Sūtra has the Buddha saying,

Oh Subhūti, because all dharmas are empty, non-existent and none are autonomous entities, vacuous lies do not hold firm; therefore all dharmas are
birthless, non-arisen, uncontrived and without views of existence (無知無
見). Furthermore Subhūti, the nature of all dharmas is without a base, without any attachments. From these causes and conditions there is no birth, no
arising, no knowing, no views of existence (無知無見).[208]

---

[207] 佛說長者女菴提遮師子吼了義經 *Fo shuo chang zhe nu An Tizhe shi zi houle yi jing,*
'Sutra spoken by the Buddha on the Clear Meaning of the Lion's Roar to An Tizhe,
daughter of an elder' (also known as the *Sutra of the Elder's Daughter* 長者子女經 or
長老子女經), translator unknown, 6th cent. It emphasises the importance of *bodhicitta*
(aspiration towards awakening) practice and shows how practitioners should overcome obstacles in order to achieve liberation. T0580.14.0964a24.

[208] T0220.06.0561a14.

The *Huayan-sūtra* says,

> The Dharma-seal of thusness is the seal of all the gates to deeds and their consequences. To come to the dharma of non-arising, abide in the place the Buddhas abides in. To contemplate the nature of non-arising is the seal of all spheres of cognition (諸境界) and all the Buddhas protect it. Arouse the resolve to dedicate oneself to awakening (發心迴向), in accord with the nature of all dharmas (法性). In accordance with the dedication, enter the uncreated dharmas, accomplished by expedient means.[209]

Due to not being awake to the meaning of only consciousness (唯心) people have yet to enter the teachings of the Ancestral Mirror, which are directed towards birthlessness. Giving rise to the pollutants of greed and delusion within true emptiness, attached to the causal situations of the objective world, because of being at odds with the cure, transmigration is its result. If it were possible to return the light within, then consciousness and the objective realm would both be quiescent. The *Zhufa Wuxing jing* says,

> If a bodhisattva sees into the realm of desire as really being ultimate reality; sees into the realm of anger as really being the ultimate reality; sees into the realm of folly as really being the ultimate reality; then all the faults incurred by karmic hindrances can finally cease.[210]

Even averagely naïve people, due to not knowing of the ultimate mark of the cessation of all dharmas [of conditioned existence], see themselves and also others are seen with this view [of unknowing], which then gives rise to intentional actions of body, speech and intention (意). They do not even see the Buddha, do not see the Dharma, do not see the Sangha, so this is not seeing any dharmas. If no dharmas are seen in the midst of all dharmas, then doubt does not arise and because doubt does not arise, then no dharma is acceptable. Because no dharma is accepted, then one's own quiescence is destroyed. As *The Inconceivable Buddha Realm Sutra* says,

---

[209] T0279.10.0128b04.

[210] 諸法無行經 *Zhufawuxing jing, Sarvadharmâpravṛtti Nirdeśa Sūtra,* 'Sutra on the karmic non-Accumulation of all Dharmas' translated by Kumārajīva (344–413). T0650.15.0753b28.

At that time the World-honoured One again addressed Mañjuśri bodhisattva: 'Oh son [of the Tathāgata], are you not fully able to realise the equality of the Dharma[211] that the Tathāgata abides in?' Mañjuśri bodhisattva answered, 'World-honoured One, I have already realised it fully.' The Buddha said, 'Oh son, what is the equality of the Dharma that the Tathāgata abides in?' Mañjuśri answered, 'World-honoured One, all worldlings giving rise to the states of greed, anger and delusion, these are the equality of the Dharma the Tathāgata abides in.' The Buddha said, 'Oh son, say, is what all worldlings who give rise to states of greed, anger and delusion the equality of all dharmas which the Tathāgata abides in?' Mañjuśri answered, 'World-honoured One, all worldlings in the Dharma of emptiness, signlessness and wishlessness give rise to greed, anger and delusion, therefore all worldlings giving rise to the states of greed, anger and delusion is just this equality of the Dharma that the Tathāgata abides in.' [429c] The Buddha said, 'Oh son, emptiness, would this be an existent dharma, in the middle of which it is said that there is greed, anger and delusion?' Mañjuśri bodhisattva answered, 'World-honoured One, emptiness is existent (空是有), therefore greed, anger and delusion also exist.' The Buddha said, 'Oh son, how could emptiness exist? Again, how could greed, anger and delusion exist?' Mañjuśri bodhisattva answered, 'World-honoured One, emptiness, because it is explained in words, it exists; greed, anger and delusion too, because of being explained in words, exist. As the Buddha has said [to his monks], "Monks! There is a nothing that is born, nothing that arises, nothing that produces, nothing that acts and there are no methods of practice; this no-birth, non-arising, non-production, non-action and no methods of practice is not non-existent. If these did not exist, then there would be no escape from birth, arising, production, action and all methods of practice. Therefore, because they exist, there is talk of emancipation. Again, in the same way, if emptiness did not exist, then there would no emancipation from greed, anger, and delusion, but because they exist, it is therefore said that there is a release from all afflictions such as anger and so forth."'[212]

---

²¹¹ *Pingdeng fa* 平等法 as seen from the standpoint of emptiness.

²¹² 文殊師利所說不思議佛境界經 *Wenshushili suoshuo busiyi fojingjie jing,* 'Sutra of Mañjuśrī's Explanation of the Inconceivable Buddha realm' translation by Bodhiruci 菩提流志 (572?–727) in 693 CE. T0340.12.0108b22. Also discussed in 瑜伽師地論

As a gatha in the *Mūlamadhyamaka-śāstra* says,

> Dharmas do not arise from Dharma
> Nor is there arising of non-[unlawful] dharmas
> From non-dharmas there is no arising
> Dharma is tantamount to non-dharmas[213]

The straightforward interpretation of the verse: dharmas actually exist, just like colour, consciousness, and so on. Non-dharmas are non-existent, such as the horns of a rabbit and so on. When dharmas are born from Dharma, it is like a mother giving birth to offspring; Dharma born from non-dharmas is like a person giving birth to a stone maiden. From non-dharmas giving rise to Dharma is like the horns of a rabbit giving birth to a man. From non-dharmas giving birth to non-dharmas is like the hairs of a turtle giving birth to the horns of a rabbit. Therefore the *Vajracchedikā prajñāpāramitā-Sūtra śastra* says,

> Again there is a consideration which says that if the Tathāgata only verified that there is nothing to be attained, [then] what the Buddha-dharma attains,[214] identity with the one is without limits (佛法得一非是無邊). Therefore a sutra says,[215] 'The Tathāgata espouses all dharmas, all are the Buddha-dharma.' What is being referred to as the Buddha-dharma? It is precisely that there is nothing to attain. There has never been a Dharma that possesses the nature of being attainable; therefore all dharmas are nothing other than the Buddha-dharma. What is everything, the all which cannot be attained to? A sutra says, 'All these dharmas are not all dharmas.' Why not? Because there is no nature of arising/birth and if there is no arising/birth then there is no [existent] nature (無性). Why the name *all dharmas* in the midst of there being no [existent] nature? Because it is a nominal

---

Yuqie shidi lun, Yogâcārabhūmi-śāstra, 'Discourse on the Stages of Concentration Practice' translated by Xuanzang 玄奘 between 646–648 CE. T1579.30.0577b19.

[213] 中觀論 *Zhongguan lun. Mūlamadhyamaka-kārikā*, translated by Kumārajīva 鳩摩羅什 in 409, with his own comments. T1564.30.0028b27. Translation tentative.

[214] 即 emended to 得, T1515.25.0894a12.

[215] E. g. T0235.08.0751b01 金剛般若波羅蜜經 and other Prajñā sutras quoted in T1515 (see next but one note).

explanation that all dharmas have no existent nature (無有性) – this is the nature of the *tathāgata-garbha*[216] of sentient beings.'[217]

Layman Pang had a verse:

> Fire burns aeons in heaven yet the gods are not heated
> Mountain mists blow around but make no sound
> Hundreds of streams compete to flow yet the ocean does not overflow
> The five famous mountain peaks, their forms are not seen
>
> Clarifying deep meditation leaves no trace
> A thousand paths exhausted, all enter the unborn[218]

Therefore it is known that all the dharmas take their form from intellect (意 *manas*), the thousand paths cause consciousness to have / produce images; a single remembered thought moment (一念) is lucid quiescence (澄寂). The ten thousand objects are empty appearance (曠然), originally the same gate to non-duality, a pointer to the definitive entry into the unborn. And so Fu Dashi talked of the path as difficult, saying,

> 'You sir do not see all the dharmas as a merely nominal postulate of emptiness – the deep meditation of no-gate is the Dharma-gate. Amongst all dharmas, consciousness is the **[430a]** master. I will now no longer obtain the source of consciousness, for, since having investigated thoroughly, I could not find it. It should be known that all dharmas are utterly without roots'.[219]

---

[216] The spiritual 'womb' where the Buddha-is / Buddha to-be is carried.

[217] 金剛般若波羅蜜經破取著不壞假名論 *Jingang bore boluomi jing po quzhe bu huai Jiaming lun, Vajracchedikā prajñāpāramitā-Sūtra śastra,* on the refutation of grasping onto the indestructible, nominally established. Composed by Guñada (?) 功德施 菩薩, translated by Divākara *et al* 683 CE. T1515.25.0894a12.

[218] 心賦注／注心賦 *Xin fu zhu/zhu xin fu,* 'Annotations on the heart's endowment' or 'Notes on consciousness in the *fu* verse form,' attributed to Master Yongming Yanshou himself. X63n1231.0103c21.

[219] Semi-legendary Fu Dashi 傅大士 (497–569). 善慧大士語錄 'Recorded Sayings of

Again, non-arising has two [aspects]. As the *Tongxin Lun*[220] says,

> The first is the absence of arising in the Dharma-nature. The ineffable principle is called Dharma, even to the nature of vacuous speech, originally of itself (自爾), is called non-arising. The second is the non-arising of conditioned arising, that is, objects appearing from consciousness and therefore not generated from other [causes]. Consciousness registers [its] objects arising, therefore [they are] not naturally existing (不自生). Every consciousness-object is different; therefore they do not arise together. The characteristic of cause is thus present, therefore not generated without a cause.

It is also said,

> First is the principle of non-arising – the perfectly accomplished nature of reality, because it originally does not arise. Second is that there is non-arising of phenomena – the mark of conditioned arising, just because it is non-arisen. [221]

As the *Zhiguan* says,

> If one were to interpret the *Diamond Sutra* by turning the meaning towards / moving on from non-arising and cross over to enter into the gate of non-abiding, [then] there are various modes of non-abiding – [such as] the gift that does not abide in form, the gift that does not abide in sound, odour and other kinds of giving. Although no dharmas abide, it is because of the non-abiding that dharmas abide in wisdom (*prajñā*), which is to enter emptiness. It is because of non-abiding of dharmas that relative worldly truth abides, which is to enter conventional existence (*or* realise the provisional 入假). It is because of the non-abiding of dharmas that ultimate reality

the Eminent Layman Shanhui Fu Dashi'. Compiled during the Tang dynasty 唐代 (618–907) by Lou Ying 樓穎 (n. d.). X69n1335.0119b02.

[220] Not extant.

[221] Recorded later in 注大乘入楞伽經 a commentary by Bao Chen 寶臣 (Song dyn. n. d.) on the *Laṅkâvatāra-Sūtra* (trans. Śikṣānanda 實叉難陀 in 700, T 672.16). T1791.39.0467b26.

(實相) abides, which is what is entered into [intellectually? 入中]. This is the wisdom of non-abiding, which is the adamantine samadhi, capable of destroying plate, stone, sand and potsherds, penetrating to the limit of the origin (本際), also like Shakyamuni entering the great quiescence-concentration of the adamantine samadhi. As for the treatises of Asaṅga and Vasubandhu, extensively discussed by Kaishan,[222] how could the meaning (意) transcend non-arising and non-abiding? If one comes to this meaning, the thousand sutras and ten thousand treatises open wide, without any obstructions. This is the first chapter in learning contemplation, of conceiving the meaning of the fundamental, the ineffable wisdom of being able to untie differences, the crucial pointer to the entry of the Way, a structure vast and great, perfectly endowed with both relative and absolute [aspects]. When one is understood, a thousand follow, the Dharma-gates unimpeded.[223]

Therefore it should be known that all of the various dharmas, all exist in accord with the unborn/non-arising nature of emptiness – existent yet non-existent; not separate from the conventional world yet ever real – non-existent yet existent; not separate from the real yet constant with the conventional world, so that magical phenomena are established but their manifestation is non-arisen. Emptiness and existence are distinct, [but] the two characteristics interpenetrate (兩相泯) and both phenomena exist. Reality and the mundane are just like this (*or* equally supple 宛爾), so that there is no arising yet no non-arising, they do not abide in the two extremes. Therefore an ancient worthy had a verse:

> Non-arising does ultimately not abide
> The myriad phenomena spread everywhere
> If an understanding of non-arising is created
> Then that is still non-arisen[224]

---

[222] I. e. Zhizang 智藏 (458–522) of Kaishan temple 開善寺, work no longer extant.

[223] 摩訶止觀 *Mohe Zhiguan*, 'The great Śamatha-Vipaśyanā [practices]' by Zhiyi 智顗 (538–597 CE), T1911.46.0084a09. This large work has been translated by Paul L. Swanson, *Clear Serenity, Quiet Insight*.

[224] T1736.36.0283a08 = 無生終不住，萬象徒流布。若作無生解，還被(被＝彼)無生顧(顧＝故)。即其義也。
T2016.48.0430a22 = 無生終不住。萬像徒流布。若作無生解。還被無生固。(被 emended to 彼﹐固 to 故).

Question: To take consciousness as the source teaching (宗), principle is necessarily the definitive, yet in accord with the world of sentient beings. Truth and falsehood are seemingly divided and cannot be identified with one another. There is an excess of [opinions on] perfect enlightenment. It is like gold and copper being smelted together – the real and the counterfeit are suddenly separated, sand and rice cooked together come to a different fruition. Not yet understood – with which is consciousness taken as the source teaching?

Answer: This is really the question, needing the consciousness of subtle consciousness (識心), for this is ineffable, difficult to know and only a Buddha can explain it. The longing for the Way exclusive to the three vehicles is in seeing that there are differences. The mistake is to point to the foolish consciousness and take it as ultimate reality – to acknowledge the errant thief as the offspring of the Tathāgata. Aeons of exhausting the family treasure (Buddha-nature), collecting the eyes of fish is taken as the production of white [**430b**] pearls – a vacuous delusion in the wisdom eye resulting in the foolish offspring being trapped in the heavy barriers of hell. Such persons, nefariously fallen, drown and see rivers of fearful waves. Playing in a decrepit house afire, forgetting hardship and forgetting exhaustion, they lie down in the long night of a great dream. Deluded in consciousness, deluded by nature, all is grasped by conceptual thinking (緣慮) creating their own life. Forgetting this true consciousness, acknowledging other sounds and forms, this then is to enter vulgar heterodox ways, ordinary folk lost in the home-life.

Even longing for the Way of the three vehicles or practising the Dharma of the Chan School (禪宗) deludes their consciousness. Holding on to the Buddha's expedient means causes the teachings to open the eight nets,[225] to avail oneself of the four correct opportunities[226] and, transcending one thought-moment, to

[225] 八網 = 網目 The 'eyes' or meshes of a net, as in the *Brahmajāla Sūtra* 梵網經. In Tiantai taxonomy the four modes of teaching (sudden, gradual, esoteric, indeterminate) 化儀四教 are likened to a great net, and the four types of methodology according to audience capacity (Hinayana, intermediate, distinct, bodhisattva) 化法四教 are likened to its meshes, following DDB, Paul Swanson.

[226] Four opportunities 四機, to refrain from all evils and to pursue all good deeds; secondly, the Hinayana way, to seek nirvana; the third is the Bodhisattva's opportunity, to put others before oneself, to be compassionate and loving; the fourth, to look at all

gallop beyond three great aeons to achieve the emptiness of a great aeon. Leaving [this] precious place, long time submerged and moulded by enclosing walls, the tracks are beset by long contradictory paths. This then is the small fruit of a limited capacity – and even this is lost to those in the Chan School (禪宗) who have not come to the meaning. Therefore the *Śūraṃgama-sūtra* says,

> The Buddha said to Ananda, 'Every living being from beginningless time, of various erroneous ways, has naturally karmic seeds, like the bunched seeds [of the Rudrashka tree].[227] None of these practitioners is capable of attaining the peerless bodhi and do not even become sravakas or pratyeka-buddhas, but all become heretic Mara kings and join Mara's retinue – all due to not knowing the two roots. Practising in error and confusion, it is like cooking with sand in the wish to produce a tasty dish. Even passing through dusty aeons they will never attain. What are these two roots? Ananda, the first is the beginningless root of birth and death; indeed you now, all sentient beings are focussed with consciousness on clinging to phenomena for the sake of their own nature. The second is beginningless bodhi (awakening) and nirvana, originally pure in essence (元清淨體), so for you of today, consciousness pure and originally luminous (識精元明) can give rise to various conditions, but those causes which are abandoned are due to various sentient beings abandoning this original clarity. Even to practise to the end of days without awakening oneself is to vainly enter the round of rebirths.'[228]

The explanation is that these two kinds of roots are just the two consciousnesses of truth and delusion. As to the first kind, the beginningless root of birth and death, it is precisely the root of ignorance. This is the deluded consciousness, initially lost in [this] one Dharma realm; not awakened, it suddenly arises

dharmas and see the true nature of the Middle Way in order to break all confusions and get out of birth and death, which is also the Buddha's opportunity.

[227] *Elaeocarpus ganitrus* tree, whose dried seeds serve Hindus and Buddhists as rosaries. The seeds stick together like the seeds of karma (!).

[228] 大佛頂如來密因修證了義諸菩薩萬行首楞嚴經, *Da foding rulai miyin xiuzheng liaoyi zhupusa wanconsciousnessg shoulengyan jing, Śūraṃgama-sūtra,* translated by Pramiti 般剌蜜帝 705 CE, widely assumed to be a text originally written in China rather than Indian (DDB). To945.19.0108b28.

and has these [deluded] thoughts. The sudden arising is really beginningless, like the appearance of flowers working on the eyeball; sleeping deeply, dreams arise. Originally no basic cause arose – not an existent determining the place of arising, for all is from erroneous thoughts; nor does it come from other extraneous conditions. From these [factors] a subtle karmic consciousness is generated, which will then give birth to future consciousness (轉識), then later evolving into a consciousness enabling the arising of a perceptual awareness of the external world (現識). The functioning of these three consciousnesses active in the external world – the karmic, the changing (evolving 轉) and the manifesting, is common to all living beings and is the beginning of clinging to internal and external phenomena, in place of consciousness's true nature. Due to this birth and death continue, which is taken as the root.

Concerning the second [kind of root], beginningless bodhi, nirvana and the originally pure essence, this is really the true consciousness, also called the innate nature of pure consciousness (自性清淨心), also called pure intrinsic awakening (清淨本覺). Because nothing arises, nothing is born; the intrinsic nature (自體) does not move, is not stained by [430c] birth and death nor purified by nirvana. The eye is pure and this pure essence is the seminal origin (精元) of the eight consciousnesses, original perfect clarity. Due to obeying the defilements, not awakening and not adhering to one's [true] nature is like sound generated in accord with the condition of an empty valley's echo. This is also true of a capacity to produce various dharmas, then immediately seeing such phenomena as split in two, with consciousness and objects mutually engendering each other. It is simply obeying the conditions of defilement or purity, the nature of the complete and ever abiding (圓常) left behind, just as water obeys the wind, creating waves. As a result, these sentient beings lose the original root and chase after the branches, ever sinking and never aware of it, experiencing the bitterness of delusion in vain. Although experiencing the bitterness of delusion, true happiness remains ever alive – one can choose to cross the stream and ascend, or sink, for the original awareness does not change, just as water creates waves yet does not lose its nature of wetness. Merely to be familiar with the changeable consciousness creating objects is due to awakening becoming delusion – and from delusion comes more delusion. Passing in vain through aeons of dust and sand, causing dreams to produce [more] dreams, in the eternal dusk the night is long. Therefore a sutra says,

It should be known that the continuum of birth and death of all sentient beings from beginningless time is wholly due to not knowing of the ever-abiding nature of the true consciousness's pure and luminous essence. Applying various erroneous concepts, these concepts are not true; therefore there is transmigration. [229]

Because of not fully understanding the immovable true consciousness but obeying the transmigrating wheel of deluded consciousness, this consciousness has no essence. The true consciousness is originally the real source without characteristics, not separated, but turning off course it brought into existence emotive and foolish concepts, like the wind giving rise to waves on a pure deep lake. Although the waves move, yet ever abiding is the immovable depth. It is like cataracts of the eye producing flowers in empty space – although flowers are present, they are connected to the nature of space. Cataracts vanished, the space is pure; waves at an end, the lake is peaceful, for there is only the one true consciousness pervading the Dharma realm. Moreover, this consciousness does not come from past time, does not live in the present time frame and does not go to cessation at a later time but, ascending and descending, is immovable. Its nature and characteristic being one and the same, then the inborn nature is received from on high, thus the Chan source teaching (宗) of the true consciousness. If the practice is left, one becomes completely entangled in Mara's snares, with separate conditions attained, all submerged in a forest of perversities. This is why the ability to mobilise deep kindness is born of manifold compassion, as when the Second Patriarch [of Chan, Huike], searching for this foolish consciousness and unable to find it, that the First Patriarch [Bodhidharma] transmitted his robe. When Ananda was clinging to this foolish consciousness, the Tathāgata then rebuked him, as the sutra says,

[The Buddha said] 'Ananda! If you now wish to know of the method for stabilising meditation (*śamatha*), wish to transcend birth and death, I now ask you again,' and immediately the Tathāgata raised his golden arm, bent his five fingers and said to Ananda, 'Do you see this now?' 'I see it,' answered Ananda. 'What do you see?' 'I see the Tathāgata raising his arm and bending his fingers, making a bright fist, dazzling my consciousness and eyes (心目),' replied Ananda. 'You and who else will see it?' asked the Buddha.

---

[229] T0945.19.0106c27.

Ananda said, 'I and the great assembly together see it.' The Buddha told Ananda, 'You answer me now, the Tathāgata bends his fingers to make a fist of light; it dazzles your consciousness and eyes. Your eyes can see but by what means does consciousness appropriate my fist of [431a] light?' Ananda said, 'The Tathāgata is now asking whether consciousness exists and if I can, with consciousness, advance to the ultimate in pursuit and so be able, by advancing, I will become conscious.' The Buddha said, 'What!! Ananda, this is not your consciousness.' Ananda, looking nervously round, left his seat and, palms together, stood up and said to the Buddha, 'This, not being my consciousness, then what should it be called?' Buddha told Ananda, 'This is the present object, a mark of delusional thinking impinging on cognition, confusing your true nature. From your beginningless time until the present life, you have taken the thief to be your son; you have lapsed from the origin ever abiding (元常) and have therefore been subject to the cycle of transmigration.' Ananda said to the Buddha, 'Oh World-honoured One, I am favoured by being a disciple of the Buddha and so a heartfelt affection (心愛) for the Buddha caused me to leave the home life. Why was my consciousness (我心) only giving reverence to the Tathāgata? And even passing through all the regions of the Ganges River, honouring various Buddhas and good, virtuous teachers, sending forth great vigour, practising all the difficult to practise dharma deeds, all was activated by this consciousness. Even allowing for slandering the Dharma and the permanent regression of good roots, again, it is wholly on account of this consciousness. If this clarification is not consciousness, then I do not possess a consciousness, am the same as earth and trees, separated from this realisation and still have nothing. Why [then] does the Tathāgata say that this is not the consciousness? I am truly fearful and this great assembly too are not without doubt. There is only this great affliction, so we beg you to grant great compassion and reveal it to those not yet awakened.'

Just at that time the World-honoured One revealed to Ananda and to the various great assemblies the wish to have their consciousness enter the patient acceptance of the Dharma of birthlessness (心入無生法忍). On the lion's seat he touched Ananda's head and said to him, 'The Tathāgatas ever discourse on the various dharmas produced as being solely manifestations of consciousness. All causes and [their] effects, [from] worlds [to] tiny specks of dust, are due to consciousness materialising essence (因心成體). Ananda, suppose that the various worlds and all that exists in them, even

grasses, leaves and threads, were questioned on their roots and origin –
in every case [they would be found] to have the essence nature (咸有體
性). Even so, it allows for emptiness as well as for the existence of names
and forms (亦有名貌); how much the more for the purified, ineffably pure
illumined consciousness! The nature of every consciousness is therefore
in itself non-existent (自無體). When you hold to a narrow, discriminative, discursive understanding of [the true] nature as necessarily being
consciousness, this consciousness then should be free from such sense
[discriminations] as colour, odour, taste, touch and their various defiled
activities, [as if these were] the separate existence of an integral nature. As
for you now, inheriting and listening to my teaching, this is then due to the
sound and the existence of discrimination. Even with the cessation of all
seeing, hearing, perception and knowing, [yet] guarded tranquilly inside, it
is still a matter of dharma-dust discriminating shadows. I do not command
you to hold on to what is not consciousness, but in your consciousness
subtle speculation, if disengaged from the object as being of the nature
of existence according to the discriminating consciousness, this then is
truly your consciousness. When the nature of discrimination [fashions] a
separate object (離塵) it lacks intrinsic nature (無體), this is objects discriminated as shadows. The dust does not abide permanently, for when it
changes or ceases, this consciousness is then still the same as the hairs of a
tortoise or the horns of a rabbit – then your Dharma-body would be tantamount to being eradicated (同於斷滅). But who then would be practising
and cultivating the patient acceptance of the birthless (unborn) Dharma?'[230]

An ancient commented that the one able to infer is just the functioning of a
deluded consciousness proliferating conceptual objects into thought, also coming to be called consciousness. Nevertheless, it is not the [431b] true consciousness. The deluded consciousness is the shadowy form of the true consciousness
above it, which is why it is said,

Your body, your consciousness, both are the ineffable clarity of true spirit (
真精) and within this ineffable consciousness phenomena appear.[231]

[230] T0945.19.0108c09.
[231] T0945.19.0110c23.

92

[But] if the shadowy forms are grasped as being true, then when the shadowy phenomena cease this consciousness is just severed. Therefore it is said if there is grasping onto the objects apprehended, it is really the same as cessation because the deluded consciousness is seizing on dust, making of it the essence. It is like the images in a mirror, bubbles on water; bewitched by the water, clinging to the waves; waves quietened, consciousness ceases. Bewitched by the mirror, clinging to the images, images ceased, consciousness disappears. When consciousness ceases it promptly becomes insight into cessation (*or the destruction of mistaken views* 斷見). If it is known that the nature of fluidity does not change (濕性不壞), that the substance of the mirror is ever bright, then the waves are [known as] originally empty, the shadowy images as original quiescence. Therefore know that objects are cognised by all the Buddhas as being everywhere empty (遍界遍空). The bodies and consciousness of average people are like shadows, like images. Clinging to the branches as being the root is to take the false for the true. When birth and death appear, then the unreal is verified. Therefore a sage of old declared,

> He sees the ore but is not cognisant of the gold
> On entering the furnace he begins to realise the mistake [232]

431b10

Question: The two consciousnesses, the deluded and the true – what is the meaning of calling each one 'consciousness'? What is 'essence'? What is 'characteristic'?

431b11

Answer: The true consciousness (真心) takes numinous awareness and silent understanding (靈知寂照) as consciousness; it is not false (不空) and its essence is non-abiding; the actual form of things as they really are is its attribute (實相為相).

The deluded consciousness takes the six dusts[233] of subjective shadows as consciousness and the lack of [true] nature (無性) for the essence – its characteristic marked by clinging to conditioned intentional thought (緣思慮). This conditioned thought is capable of cognising and clearly awakening to the delud-

---

[232] Not extant.

[233] Or six thieves, i. e., the five senses and thought.

ed consciousness but is without essence, so is merely impinged by objects [from the six senses], following objects existent and non-existent. When an object comes, it registers [in the senses]; object gone, then it disappears. Due to the object there is arising [of it in consciousness] yet the whole object *is* consciousness; again, because consciousness cognises objects, so the whole consciousness is the objective/subjective [field], but each [object] lacks intrinsic nature (無自性) – it is only cause and effect. Therefore the *Dharma-phrase Sutra* says,

> Blazing light is without water
> It is solely yang energy (*qi* 氣)
> In yin there is no colour
> It is solely conditioned *qi* [234]

When it is hot there is the energy of burning, due to the sun shining brightly; seen from a distance it resembles water but is simply generated from perception; it is only sun energy, nothing more. This vacuous, deluded form of consciousness is also just like this. It takes the functioning of its various senses (自業) as primary cause; mother and father is the external objective condition, their uniting resembles the manifest form of consciousness. But it is merely conditioned energy. Therefore it is said in the *Sutra of Perfect Enlightenment*, 'Deludedly discerning the subjective shadow of the six dusts (senses) as being the intrinsic nature of consciousness (自心性).'[235] Know therefore that this is consciousness that can infer; but if there were no causes and conditions then it (consciousness) would not produce its arising, for the production is exclusively from conditions. The dharmas produced by conditions are all impermanent, just like shapes in a mirror, without essence and completely due to external phenomena, like the moon [reflected] on water; not real, therefore vacuous projections in revolving nothingness (虛現空輪). To take this as the true is the extreme of foolishness. As a result there is rejoicing in attachments, without any basis. Yet the seven abodes of consciousness are vast. [236]

---

[234] Four Chinese translations of the *Dhammapada*, T210–213; but the quote is from T2901.85.1433b10, a Dunhuang manuscript, 法句經, not in T210–213.

[235] A quote from one of the numerous later commentaries but not found in the *Sutra of Perfect Enlightenment* T842.

[236] 1) Sentient beings with a variety of bodies and ideas (humans and some gods); 2) beings with a variety of bodies but identical ideas; 3) with identical bodies but a

The Second Patriarch [of Chan, Huike] understood but could not give rise to one word in agreement with the Way; so then the Second Patriarch beseeched [Bodhidharma] concerning his restless consciousness's association with objects (緣慮不安之心), and then he promptly realised that the true consciousness pervades everywhere. Awakened to this as the Chan teaching, he (Huike) was then the first to continue [after Bodhidharma] and assume the patriarchal seat.

Ananda was able to overcome his delusional consciousness because the Tathāgata refuted it, even to detailing one by one the exhaustive analysis and penetration of the five skandhas, [431c] the six bases of the senses,[237] the twelve sense fields (six senses and their objects), the eighteen compositional elements of cognition[238] and the seven great elements,[239] that they are only empty and none have any self-nature. Since it is not the existence of causal results merging self and other, it is also not naturally engendered without a cause. Being all mental chatter, conscious suppositions and discriminations – because of all this he (Ananda) suddenly awakened to the wonderful clarity of the true consciousness, so that all the great assembly came to this consciousness and all praised the Buddha in unison. Therefore the sutra says,

At that time Ananda, together with the whole great assembly, received the Buddha, the Tathāgata's wondrously subtle disclosure of the teaching. Their own consciousness serene (蕩然), attained without impediments, so that each one in the great assembly knew for themselves that consciousness pervades the ten directions. They saw the emptiness of the ten directions, just like seeing leaves in the palm of one's hand. The various existing things in all the worlds, all is in fact the ineffably luminous, original consciousness of awakening (bodhi). Consciousness's essence is everywhere complete, contained in the ten directions. To look back and contemplate the body, born from mother and father, that [too] seems as if there were only emptiness in the ten directions of space. A gust of wind blows one

variety of ideas; 4) with identical bodies and ideas (universally pure gods); 5) beings belonging to the first formless realm, beyond form and ideas, the sphere of limitless space; 6) beings in the sphere of limitless consciousness; 7) beings in the sphere of the third formless realm, the sphere of nothingness. DDB.

[237] The six are the qualities and effects of the six organs of sense.

[238] The six sense faculties 六根, their six objects 六塵 and the six consciousnesses 六識.

[239] Earth, water, fire, wind, space, sight and consciousness (from T0945.19.0119a24).

particle of dust and whether it survives or perishes, it is like a floating bubble arising and ceasing in the great ocean deep, without consequence (無從). Realising this for themselves they recovered the original ineffable consciousness, ever abiding without ceasing. Bowing to the Buddha with palms together, gaining what they had never had before, [Ananda], in front of the Tathāgata, recited a gatha in praise of the Buddha,

> Immovable Honoured-one, profoundly holding to the good
> Sovereign of heroic valour (首楞嚴王), rare in the worlds
> Extinguishing my countless aeons of topsy-turvy thinking
> Not passing vast aeons to attain the Dharma-body[240]

This is just the same as the First Patriarch [Bodhidharma] pointing directly to the human heart (consciousness), to see into its nature and become Buddha.

431c16

Question: What is the textual precedent for the defining activity of an awakened consciousness (真心)?

431c16

Answer: It is said in the *Sutra of the World Upholder*,

> The bodhisattva contemplates consciousness (觀心).[241] Within consciousness there are no characteristics of consciousness; this consciousness from the very beginning is not born, does not arise; its nature is forever pure. Adventitious afflictive stains of defilement there are and so there is discrimination but consciousness does not know consciousness, does also not see consciousness. Why is it so? Because consciousness is empty, [true] nature is itself empty; therefore a root does not exist. This consciousness is not a definite thing (法), therefore a definite thing cannot be obtained. This consciousness does not possess a Dharma. Whether combined or dispersed, this consciousness can never be obtained at any time.[242] This consciousness has no form and none are able to see it; consciousness cannot see itself,

---

[240] T0945.19.0119b03.
[241] The phrase does not appear in T0482 but in the alternative translation T0481.14.0634b27.
[242] 是心 前際不可得 後際不可得 中際不可得.

96

nor does it know its own nature. Even the people of former times did not differentiate between 'this is consciousness, this is not consciousness,' but well understood consciousness to be without the characteristics of arising: they penetrated consciousness as the nature of the unborn. Why is this so? Consciousness has neither a fixed nature nor of definite characteristics, nor is it something truly existing. It does not even acquire the characteristics of mental defilements (心垢相) nor does it acquire the characteristics of mental purity. Quite simply this is known as consciousness, its characteristic ever pure.[243]

The *Mahāprajñāparamītā-Sūtra* says,

Although there is nothing to grasp in any dharma, still, all deeds can be achieved.[244]

The explanation: if one's own consciousness is understood, there are no affairs that cannot be undertaken, or rather, grasping delusionary phenomenal objects is to become inwardly forever dissatisfied with self. Therefore the *Vajrasamādhi-Sūtra* says,

The bodhisattvas contemplate the characteristic of the original nature, [432a] referring to it as complete in itself; a thousand thoughts, ten thousand ruminations offend the principle of the Way. Followers work up disturbances and lose the sovereign original consciousness.[245]

The commentary says,

Of incalculable efficacious power (功德) is just this one consciousness – the one consciousness as the host, so it is called the sovereign consciousness (心王). Arising and ceasing in turmoil is contrary to this sovereign

---

[243] 持世經 *Chishi jing*, 'Sutra of the World Upholder' translated by Kumārajīva 鳩摩羅什 (early 5th cent) a dialogue between the Buddha and the bodhisattva World-Upholder 持世菩薩. T0482.14.0658c02.

[244] T0220.05.0210a15.

[245] T0273.09.0366c21.

consciousness and would preclude a return [to the one consciousness] – so is called lost.[246]

Furthermore, concerning consciousness, it has full command over the various dharmas and of all it is the most superior, for there is not a single dharma not included in it. As for the sovereign, he unites and governs the four seas, receives homage from the eight wastelands and there is not one of his subjects who is not a minister, which is why the *As-if-Samādhi Were Illusion Sutra* says,

Do not seek all the teachings for one's own sake[247]

and the *Sutra of Advancing to the Great Vehicle's Skilful Means* says,

Those who truly contemplate thusness (reality) ponder the nature of consciousness; that it neither comes to be nor ceases to be; does not abide in seeing, hearing, feeling or knowing and is forever free from all conceptual discriminations.'[248]

432a09

Question: Consciousness is able to become Buddha, consciousness produces a sentient being and with insight into the true/awakened consciousness (真心) one therefore becomes a Buddha. As a result of grasping onto the deluded consciousness one then becomes a sentient being. When one becomes a Buddha there is a full endowment of the five eyes[249] of perfect penetration, without the defiled outflows of the five skandhas, therefore a sutra says, 'Eliminate the impermanent forms and acquire the permanent form,'[250] and another says, 'The

---

[246] 金剛三昧經論 *Commentary on the Geumgang sammae gyeong, Vajrasamādhi-Sūtra,* T0273 by the Korean scholar-monk Wonhyo 元曉 (617–686). T1730.34.0969c12. See Buswell, Robert E, Jr. *The Formation of Chan Ideology.*

[247] 如幻三昧經 *Ruhuan sanmei jing,* 'The As-if-Samādhi were Illusion Sutra' translation by Dharmarakṣa 竺法護 (239–316) (名 emended to 爲). T0342.12.0147c13.

[248] Not a quote from 進趣大乘方便經 (佛說大方廣善巧方便經 T0346 (Nj. 926) but from 占察善惡業報經 *Zhancha shan'e yebao jing,* 'Sutra on the Divination of the Effect of Good and Evil Actions' assumed to have been originally composed in East Asia (DDB). T0839.17.0908b16.

[249] The earthly eye, heavenly eye, wisdom eye, Dharma eye and Buddha eye.

[250] T1763.37.605b04.

ineffable form is a deeply imbued and permanently abiding repose,'[251] and yet again, 'The skilled are able to distinguish all dharma phenomena,'[252] so why say that the true consciousness that does not abide in seeing, hearing, feeling and knowing is forever free from all conceptual thinking?

432a14

Answer: When the deluded consciousness sees and hears it is necessarily due to nominal (provisional) causes and conditions (假因緣) capable of producing their arising and so it is said that 'the eye is endowed with (具) the nine conditions for arising'[253] and so forth. When associated causes harmoniously unite into formless emptiness, then the nature of views/opinions has no basis to acquire manifestation, and so it is with the five root faculties – all rely on causal conditions to arise. This then is the coming together of various conditions and their arising. Conditions dispersed, they cease. There is no controller-self (無自 主宰), for ultimately the [true] nature is empty, as a gatha in the *Laṅkâvatāra-Sūtra* says,

> Consciousness is a skilful son
> Meaning, as if skilled in harmony
> The five consciousnesses are the companions
> Deluded conceptions are observed with many skills[254] (妄想觀 技眾)

It is like a person singing and dancing; skill established, moving in response to the others' beat. If the beat is slow then his pace is slow; if the beat is fast then his pace is fast – and the five root faculties are also like this, they simply change by following their inclinations, as it is said, 'the [afflicted] body is not

---

[251] 維摩經玄疏 *Weimojing xuanshou,* 'Profound Commentary on the Vimalakīrti Sutra' by Zhiyi 智顗 (538–597). T1777.38.0551a26.

[252] T1736.36.0232b01.

[253] Listed as 識中眼識一種藉九緣生： emptiness 空; brightness/light 明; root 根; object 境; focussing attention 作意; root 根本; defilement and purity 染淨; to distinguish [forms] 分別; potentiality/seed 種子 in T1791.39.0500b21.

[254] 楞伽阿跋多羅寶經 *Lengqie abaduoluo Baojing, Laṅkâvatāra-Sūtra,* Guṇabhadra's 求那跋陀羅 (394–468) partial translation. T0670.16.0510c19.

99

the activity of (the seat of) recollection (身非念輪)²⁵⁵ but recollection (隨念) is transformative.²⁵⁶ How so? Should the stage of conceptualising consciousness (意地) arise, the body's activity begins to function. Should conceptualising consciousness cease, then the sense faculties and their objects become quiescent. The true consciousness then is not that [of a conceptualising consciousness] but is ever bright, ever present – a ring of iron would not be able to conceal its radiance, for it pervades the three thousand great chiliocosms (遍界) and the all-pervasive void. The dome of the blue-green firmament cannot cover its essence; neither pure nor impure, myriad dharmas cannot hide its true nature. Non-abiding, resting on nothing, afflictions and toil cannot change its nature. How could it effuse its radiance by relying on old afflictions? In response to objects, a knowing arises, a naturally void and quiescent, numinous awareness, profound and limitless. Therefore the *Śūraṃgama-sūtra* says,

> The Buddha said, 'Ananda! The six sense organs are just like this – due to those waking up there is perfectly clear consciousness; but having lost their seminal clarity (精了), sticky attachments (黏妄) emit a radiance [as objects]. This is why you are at present separated from the hidden, separated from clarity and without the existence of an organ of insight you are separated from action, separated from tranquillity. Originally there was no quality of listening, [432b] no penetration, no obstruction; the nature of perceiving odours had not arisen; change was not, nor tranquillity and there was never anything that had emerged, nor anything separate or united; feeling and touch originally were not, nor was there cessation or arising, or realisation of a peaceful refuge (安寄). You just do not comply with action and quietness, with gathering and separating, tranquillity and change, passing through and closing up, with cessation and birth, the hidden and the apparent – all these are the twelve characteristics of existence. Then, to pull out one root, liberated from attachment, [affliction] is overcome within and overcome, it is the return to the originally true. Emitting a shining lu-

---

²⁵⁵ One of three wheels 三輪; wheel refers to the three kinds of activity (physical, verbal, and mental) of the Buddhas and bodhisattvas who preach the Dharma and are aware of their listeners' capacities and adjust the content of their discourse accordingly; 念輪 = 憶念輪, recollection, mindfulness. Or, the three wheels are illusion, karma, and suffering.

²⁵⁶ A phrase in T0721.17.0248b24 where 'mindfulness' is explained.

cency from the source, the shining nature emits clarity [of awakening]. All the rest of the five attachments should be extirpated for complete liberation. Knowledge and insight do not arise from old afflictions; awakening does not obey [those] roots. Rely on the faculty of clarity to manifest and based on this, [all] six sense faculties will serve each other.

'Ananda, do you not know that in this assembly today, Aniruddha[257] sees without eyes, that Upananda[258] hears without ears; the goddess of the Ganges[259] smells odours without a nose; arrogant monk Gavāṃpati[260] got to know the taste [of the Buddha's discourse] with a different language and *śūnyatā*, the Deity of Emptiness,[261] acquired [the sense of] touch without the possession of a body? From the emanations of the Tathāgata a reflective light causes a momentary appearance, manifesting then as the quality of wind, its essence originally non-existent. All who attain total meditative cessation[262] and listeners (*śrāvakas*) who have achieved quiescence, such in the assembly as Mahākāśyapa, who a long time ago eliminated the past-consciousness-element[263] – they have perfected a clarity of realisation (了知) not due to the production of thought (心念). Ananda! If now all your roots have been pulled out, then the lustrous inside emits a glow. It is like floating dust and in a container world [where all things are only considered as utilisable (器世)] all forms transform, like the melting away of ice in hot

---

[257] Aniruddha (Anuruddha Thera), known for his possession of the divine eye, was a first cousin and one of the ten principal disciples of Śākyamuni. For his biography see DPPN: I, 85. Upananda is one of eight great dragon kings mentioned in the *Lotus Sutra*.

[258] 跋難陀龍 *Banan tuolong*.

[259] 殑伽神女 *Qingjia shennü*.

[260] 驕梵鉢提 *Jiaofan boti*, *Gavāṃpati*, monk mentioned in the *Mahāprajñāpāramitā-Sūtra* and *Lotus Sutra*. In a previous lifetime he held an arrogant attitude toward a monk, and as a punishment, was reborn with a condition of constant movement of the mouth. He became a follower of the Buddha as an attempt to overcome this condition (Muller, DDB).

[261] 舜若多神 *Shunruoduo shen*.

[262] Skt. *nirodha-samāpatti*, only attained by those non-returners who do not rely on bare insight but have destroyed the cankers, VSM: 702, trans. Nyanatiloka – but see Dan Lusthaus, *Buddhist Phenomenology*, esp. pp. 134–151 and postscript, 152–3.

[263] 'Past sense consciousness,' as basis for and one of the 六根; see DDB: 意根.

water. You should be mindful and change to the unexcelled awareness/perception (無上知覺).

'Ananda, with those worldly persons it is the case that collective views are from the sight [of objects], but if they cause a premature closure [of the eyes], then the mark of darkness appears before them – the six roots become beclouded (黯然), heads resembling feet. Those persons follow the outside with their actions, distorting it. Although they do not see – head and feet in complete contradiction – speculative thought (知覺) is the same; conditioned seeing causes the light to darken, becoming absence of insight and not being clear-sighted there is no natural blossoming forth; then none of the marks of darkness will ever be able to fade.

'Once the root afflictions have disappeared, does awakening not become the perfectly sublime?'[264]

The explanation is: *It is like those worldly people whose collective views are from the sight [of objects]* – this is primarily the understanding of mundane views; it is not [clear] vision, not insight (觀).
If [mundane views] cause a premature closure [of the eyes] then nothing will be seen – and so on with the ear and the five faculties.
Those people following the external forms with their hands (actions), *distorting them* – despite not depending on the [physical] eye it is also [necessary] to know [reality] for oneself; this applies even more to true [in]sight, which does not rely on external objects.
As for *seeing, causally conditioned, is to be reasonably understood* (因明) *as darkness turning into the absence of seeing* – this refers to worldly vision, necessarily dependant on the causal conditions of light and dark. When the afflicted root faculties join harmoniously then they turn into seeing.
As for *without [worldly vision] it is not a clear natural blossoming forth* – this is precisely the time of directly clarifying the true view of reality. The nature of insight is not the eye and since it does not belong to the eye, again, how would it be if the dark roots of affliction would give off a spurious light? Then it would be the clarity of not being clear, the seeing of no seeing.
The natural quiescence of numinous knowing, how could this ever suffer interruption? Furthermore, light and darkness are illusory mirages of the world whose characteristics are to appear and disappear. Again, how could it be cov-

---

[264] T0945.19.0123b20.

ered up? Therefore, clarity cannot clarify [it], nor can darkness darken [it] and so it is said *then none of the marks of darkness can ever obscure* [it]. [**432c**] The true nature is innate – should it not be considered perfectly wondrous? So a student asked a former worthy, 'What is the great compassion of a thousand hands and eyes (Avalokitêśvara)?' Answer: 'It is like someone touching [your] pillow in the night.'

432c03

Question: Where is the textual precedent for the defining activity of deluded consciousness (妄心)?

432c03

Answer: The *Prajñāpāramitā-Sūtra of the Ruler Pravara-deva* says,

> The Buddha said that the bodhisattvas coursing in the perfection of wisdom mindfully (念心) produce this reflection: 'this consciousness of impermanence is yet referred to as eternally abiding; suffering is called happiness; the absence of a self is called a self and impurity is called purity. Many are the actions that do not last, sudden diseases shift and change, afflicted roots are all gates to unfortunate destinies; defilements – causal conditions – are ruination to the good path. The sovereign of craving, anger and delusion, this is not to be trusted. Among all dharmas consciousness is the most excellent. If consciousness is truly familiar and comprehends all the many dharmas, that everything in the world is created consciousness; that consciousness is not the view of a self and whether good or whether bad, all arises from consciousness. Consciousness-nature spins round like a fire-wheel, easily turning like a horse and able to burn like a fire, or it violently arises like water.' If contemplated in this way, then awareness (念) does not move, does not follow the operations of consciousness but has consciousness follow and is able to subdue it; then all the dharmas are subdued.[265]

---

[265] 勝天王般若波羅蜜經 *Shengtianwang bore boluomi jing, Suvikrāntavikrāmi-pariprcchā-prajñāpāramitā-Sūtra,* a *prajñaparamitā* text taught in Rājagṛha 王舍城 to Pravara-deva-rāja (His Most Excellent Divine Majesty) Translation by Upaśūnya 月婆首那, an Indian, son of a king of 優禪尼 Udyāna/Ujjayinī in central India. Worked

In the *Mahāparanirvāṇa-Sūtra*,

> The Buddha said, 'Oh son of a good family! Consciousness: if it were permanent (unchanging), then it would also be impossible to repeatedly distinguish the variety of colours – so-called blue, yellow, red, white or purple. Oh Good son, if consciousness were unchanging, then all recollection of dharmas ought not to be forgotten. Good son, if consciousness were unchanging, then no recollection of the dharma should be forgotten. Oh Good son, if consciousness were unchanging, then whatever is read or recited should not accumulate. Once again Good son, if consciousness were unchanging, it should not talk in terms of what has been done, of what is being done or of what will be done. Were there to exist a 'has been done,' an 'is being done' or a 'will be done,' then you should know that this consciousness is definitely not unchanging. Good son, if consciousness were unchanging, then there would be no hatred or affection, neither enmity nor goodwill. If consciousness were unchanging, then one could not say 'mine' or 'yours' or whether there is death or birth. If consciousness were unchanging, then although there would be something to be done, it would not accrue. Good son, with this meaning it should be known that the nature of consciousness is in each case distinct and it should be known that it is impermanent.[266]

Further,

> What is the actual example [for this]? It is as explained in the sutras; the nature of sentient beings' consciousness is likened to that of macaque monkeys – the nature of macaque monkeys is to let go of one [thing] to seize another [thing]. The nature of sentient beings' consciousness is likewise so – attaching to things of form, sound, odour, taste and touch, without for one instant staying with them – this is cited as the actual example.[267]

It can be verified that the actual consciousness of living beings is like that of monkeys in their abode in the high trees – ceaselessly climbing up and down; or,

in Ye 鄴 538–541, then settled in Nanjing 542–546; wandered China under the Chen 陳; was active in Jiangzhou 江州 in 565. Muller/Lancaster, DDB. T0231.08.0697c05.

[266] T0375.12.0687c26.

[267] T0375.12.0781c05.

just like a copious flood of mud flowing rapidly here and there without obstruction; or like a magician travelling around various assemblies, where name and form are all illusory. When a clever child goes out onto the playground there is no reality (distinction) between the root and the branches. Therefore the *Basis of Mindfulness of the True Dharma Sūtra* says that,

> Furthermore, those monks then meditatively investigate the monkey-[like] consciousness as if seeing into monkey, likening it to those monkeys ceaselessly restless and agitated [among] various trees and branches, [in] forests of flowers and fruits and so on. In mountain valleys and cliff grottos, going about here and there, circulating unobstructedly – the monkey-[like] consciousness is also like this. Five paths are to be distinguished,[268] like various kinds of forests: the [realms of the] hells, animals and hungry ghosts – all paths resembling those trees. Living beings are immeasurable, like the many branches; desire is like the flowers and leaves. They pick and choose, desiring sounds, smells, tastes and so on, as if these were so many fruits. Moving through the mountains of the three worlds, their bodies are like storage caves, circulating without obstructions, it is the monkey consciousness. This monkey consciousness ever moves through [the realms of] the hells, the hungry ghosts, the animals and the land of birth and death.
>
> And so, those monks rely on meditative investigation of consciousness of a clever child as if seeing into the clever child. As that clever child takes up various musical instruments in the playground, creating all kinds of games, so is this consciousness of a clever child too. All kinds of activities are transformed by clothing. Those who play in the market place are referred to as being of the five stages of the path. Various adornments, various causes and conditions, all kinds of musical instruments are referred to as the realm of self (自境界). The clever child's play is the play of birth and death. Consciousness is a clever child with many games, without beginning or end, long [rounds] of birth and death.
>
> Furthermore, those monks rely on meditative investigation of the consciousness as a fish deep in the mud, as if seeing deep into the mud. Were fish, deep in the river's mud, to experience the blocked river's waters suddenly awash with confusing waves, the depths flowing rapidly, it would be

---

[268] 五道 – hell-beings, hungry ghosts, animals, human beings and gods (excluding asuras).

difficult [for them] to move about. The river might be able to float every kind and number of trees, its power violent and fast-moving, impossible to stop. Mountain streams and rivers, precipitous, fast and highly unpleasant and those fish in the mud, would they be able to enter, to leave, able to move about or stay? Consciousness's deep mud is also just so. In the desire realm, the river is swift and violent, the waves chaotic. Can one leave, can one enter, move about or stay? [269]

The *Mahāprajñāpāramitā-śāstra* says,

It is as the Buddha taught, 'Ordinary people sometimes know that the body is impermanent but are incapable of knowing that consciousness is impermanent. Supposing there would be people maintaining that the body possesses permanence, a seeming contradiction on account of taking consciousness as permanent – this would be a huge confusion. Why? The body is present for perhaps ten or twenty years, this consciousness passes day after day, the birth and death of thought after thought, each one different, never ceasing.[270]

'Longing for the arising of a different birth, longing for the cessation of a different death seems an illusory business, truly unobtainable. Therefore, due to measureless causes and conditions, to know that consciousness is impermanent, this is called the base of mindfulness. A practitioner ponders, "To whom does this consciousness belong? Who causes this consciousness?" After contemplation, no master is seen to be present and the causes and conditions of all dharmas, being in unison, are therefore not autonomous. Not being autonomous, there is then, no self-nature. There being no self-nature, there is therefore no 'I' (self). If there is no 'I' then who would cause there to be consciousness?'[271]

The *Zhiguan* says that a single thought arising is the conceptualising conscious-

---

[269] 正法念處經 *Saddharma-smṛty-upasthāna-Sūtra, Zhengfa nianchu jing,* 'The Basis of Mindfulness of the True Dharma Sutra,' translation by Gautama Prajñāruci 瞿曇般若流支 (mid. 6th cent CE). To721.17.024a14.

[270] Following Yanshou, T2016.48.0433a22, not T1509.25.0200b22 which is slightly different.

[271] T1509.25.0200b20.

ness (慮知 *citta*); it follows good and bad, giving rise to the path of ten kinds of moral behaviours (十道).[272]

The First – if this consciousness is ever concentrated on greed, anger and delusion, gathering them and not turning [to awakening], extirpating them will not succeed. As the days pass into months, those giving rise to the most virulent ten unwholesome behaviours, likened to the five *ṣaṇḍhilā*[273] – this evinces a hellish consciousness walking the path of a fiery destiny.

The Second – if this consciousness is ever concentrated on the desire for many followers, like the ocean swallowing up rivers, like fire burning firewood, giving rise to a middle level of the ten unwholesome behaviours, likened to Devadatta tempting the assembly,[274] this evinces the animal consciousness walking a blood-smeared path.

The Third – if this consciousness is ever concentrated on the desire to obtain name and fame far and wide, to be praised and admired, then there is no real inner virtue and compared to the good and noble, it is false, giving rise to a low-level of the ten unwholesome behaviours, likened to Mākandika.[275] This evinces consciousness of a demon walking a razor-sharp path of swords.

The Fourth – if this consciousness is ever concentrated on superiority over others and cannot tolerate the lowly, then the treasures of others is made light of, likened to a kite flying high and gazing below. Outwardly extolling benevolence, righteousness, propriety, wisdom and faith, it gives rise to a low-level good consciousness walking the path of the Asuras.

The Fifth – if this consciousness is ever concentrated on rejoicing in worldly pleasures, secure in its scented body, pleased with its foolish conscious-

---

[272] What Zhiyi actually says is that the Dao has commonalities and differences which he now briefly summarises as ten 道亦有通有別今亦簡之略為十. T1911.46.0004a24. Yanshou's 十道 is misleading.

[273] The five bad monks who died, went to the hells, and were reborn as *ṣaṇḍhilās* or imperfect males (lacking organs of reproduction).

[274] Śākyamuni's cousin, who joined the sangha after hearing a discourse of the Buddha. Eight years before the death of the Buddha, he plotted his cousin's death with the intent of taking control of the Buddhist movement.

[275] Mākandika, a Brahmin who appears as a debate opponent in the *Da Zhidu lun* (T1509). The Buddha judges him to be holding to false views.

ness, this gives rise to a middle-level good consciousness walking a human path.

The Sixth – if this consciousness is ever concentrated on the awareness of the three bad sufferings being many (hells, hungry ghosts and animals), that amongst humans, sufferings and joys alternate with the pure joy of the heavenly realms, then by means of the joy of heaven the crude is subdued; this is the superior level of consciousness walking a heavenly path.

The Seventh – if this consciousness is ever concentrated on the desire to have great power over body, speech and consciousness and to actually realise and quell them, so that they obey, this evinces consciousness of a lord of the desire realm walking in the path of Mara (death [of desire]).

The Eighth – if this consciousness is ever concentrated on the desire to obtain keen awareness, correct discernment, high ability and bold sagacity, reflecting intelligently the whole world of the ten directions, this evinces the consciousness of worldly wisdom, walking the path of Nigrantha.[276]

The Ninth – if this consciousness ever concentrates on the five afflictions and the six desires, joy in the outside [world] is rather weak, [whilst] the happiness of the third *dhyāna* stage of meditation[277] resembles a rock spring, its joy internally heavy, this evinces a noble consciousness walking the path of form and no-form.

The Tenth – if this consciousness ever concentrates on the knowledge of the cycles of good and bad that ordinary people indulge in and the sages berate vociferously because pure wisdom destroys the bad, as pure wisdom comes from pure meditation and pure meditation from pure precepts. Just these three dharmas are like hunger and thirst – this evinces a consciousness without any outflows (afflictions) walking the path of the two vehicles (*śrāvaka* and *pratyekabuddha*).

These ten [states of the] consciousness [mentioned] above might initially give rise to either a wrong (非) [state of] consciousness or to a right (是) [state of] consciousness, or a right and a wrong [state of] consciousness might arise together. The simile is of an elephant, a fish and wind simultaneously muddying the water of a pond. The elephant symbolises the various wrong [views] arising from the outside. The fish symbolises internal

---

[276] Nirgrantha, known as Jina (the Victor) and Mahāvīra (the Great Hero), founder of the Jains.

[277] The highest 'paradise' of form.

contemplation which is weak because it is moved by opposite poles (inner and outer). The wind symbolises inside and outside consciousness, contaminants in turbid harmony. The first nine states of consciousness are in [the world of] birth and death, like silk worms entangled in their own [cocoons]. The latter [tenth] state of consciousness is nirvana, like a roebuck solitarily leaping about. Even though liberation is attained for oneself, the Buddha-dharma is not yet attained – neither the one nor the other, meaning, both [steps one to nine and step ten of the path of ten kinds of moral behaviours] are to be omitted (雙簡).[278]

The clear acknowledgement of the three worlds is nothing other than reasoning – merely the arising of a deluded consciousness; it is the root of the eight errors,[279] making a hideaway cave away from the four raging streams,[280] fast as a flash of lightning, fierce as a mad wind. Even a glance causes the wearisome afflictions to arise, quick as a great river's explosive force of water, suddenly bringing to life the five desires,[281] like a fast-spinning fire-wheel.[282] Therefore the makeup of the four Maras[283] spurs on the ten defilements,[284] sinking [the victims] into the riverbed of the two deaths (ordinary and Buddhistic), throwing them into the flames of the eight sufferings.[285] Intoxicated and confused about the pearl within them, in vain passing through hardships and dangers, the

---

[278] T1911.46.0004a25. This passage also translated by Paul Swanson, *Clear Serenity, Quiet Insight,* pp 139–145.

[279] Permanence, happiness, self and purity and their opposites.

[280] Desire, existence, ignorance, false views.

[281] Desires arising from the five senses.

[282] Spin a burning stick and it looks like a ring of fire – illusion.

[283] 四魔 *si mo.* Four Māra-enemies (demons) that make trouble for sentient beings: the demon of ill desires; the demon of the aggregates; the five elemental aggregates of body, perception, conception, volition, and consciousness; the demon of death; the demon named *Paranirmita-vaśavartin,* who is the king of the sixth heaven in the world of desire and who tries to prevent living beings from doing good.

[284] Ten defilements, ten negative tendencies; ten afflictions: The first five, which are characteristic of those of developed religious sensitivity are: view of self, extreme view, mistaken view, view of attachment to views, and view of attachment to the precepts. The second five, which are characteristic of those of undeveloped religious sensitivity are: desire, hatred, ignorance, pride, and doubt.

[285] 八苦 *ba ku.* La naissance, la vieillesse, la maladie, la mort, la séparation d'avec ce que

treasure on the forehead submerged in struggle, emptiness laments for itself – all this because of a deluded consciousness misled about this true awakening. Ultimately there is nothing to lose. There is an indication in the writings: as [mentioned] above, relying on what has been taught, the two consciousnesses of the true and the false are relative meanings, seemingly different, yet they return to the [same] original teachings (宗) and are not different. Why is this so? The true consciousness is, in a general sense, the essence of principle; the deluded consciousness is based on characteristics and functions. Now, taking the reality principle as being always consciousness, it cannot acquire the characteristics of consciousness, for consciousness is ever the principle [itself], whose characteristic is that it is consciousness that does not move / change. It is like water just being waves – it does not acquire the characteristic of waves; waves are just this water, without contradicting the characteristic of waves.

Therefore movement and stillness have no limits, nature and characteristics are of one origin. It is just ordinary consciousness that is the Buddha-consciousness (當凡心而是佛心). Contemplating worldly truth then becomes absolute truth, which is why the *Huayan Jing* says that the bodhisattva Mahāsattva contemplates all dharmas by taking consciousness as the intrinsic nature and thus abides [in it].[286] When subsuming the object as consciousness, it is the conventionally ultimate truth. The intrinsic nature of consciousness is the true nature (thusness), the ultimate meaning of the ultimate truth and thus it abides. Although [the ultimate truth has] nothing to acquire, yet there are expedient means; both illuminate the absolute and the conventional. Therefore, without abiding they abide.

End of Fascicle Three

l'on aime, la réunion avec ce que l'on n'aime pas, ne pas obenir ce que l'on recherche, le cinq agrégats d'attachements. Paul Swanson, DDB.

[286] T0279.10.0119a01.

Records from the Ancestral Mirror

Fascicle Four

Now there are those who speak of the dharma of consciousness, but say, what is consciousness, what is the dharma of mental functions (心法)?

Answer: To understand the afflictions from the perspective of sameness (通相) – this is called the ruler of consciousness and because it is originally the one fundamental consciousness (本一心); it is the source of all the dharmas. Those who grasp at the distinctive characteristics of the afflictions are referred to as analysing (數) the dharmas and because of their innate nescience are therefore perplexed concerning the undifferentiated equality of thusness (平等性). The *Madhyānta-vibhāga* says

> If the afflictions are understood from the perspective of sameness, it is called consciousness. To grasp the distinctive characteristics of afflictions is called the dharma of mental functions (心法). [287]

Question: This dharma of the one (universal) consciousness, how many interpretations (義) does it generate?

Answer: The dharma of consciousness has in general four interpretations. The *first* concerns the situation (事): it differentiates according to / following objects / circumstances – seeing, hearing, cognition and knowing. The *second* interpretation concerns Dharma: the format of the discussion being only with respect to the Buddhist categories of birth and death – with these two interpre-

---

[287] This does not seem to be a quotation from T1600.31, 辯中邊論, *Madhyānta-vibhāga, Bian zhongbian lun,* 'Analysis of the Middle and the Extremes' translated by Xuanzang 玄奘 (in 661). The quote is found in 起信論疏 *Qixin lunshu,* 'Commentary on the Awakening of Faith' by the Korean monk Wonhyo 元曉 (617–686), T1844.44.0209c14.

tations – that discussed as mundane and it therefore exists, but if, simply stated, it is based on the absolute (thusness), it does not exist. The *third* interpretation concerns principle: to thoroughly investigate emptiness. **[434a]** The *fourth* interpretation concerns reality and the discussion of its original nature – that there is only the reality of the Tathāgata's true Dharma (如來藏法).

434a01

Question: Within the four interpretations of consciousness, the first two interpretations are conditioned by consciousness thinking delusively, whilst the last two concern the ever-abiding true consciousness. In short, the true consciousness is then the original nature's ineffable investigations of the principle of emptiness (空寂). Given the absence of an enumeration, there are no further indications, as it only involves the seemingly deluded consciousness's seeing and hearing. It is said of birth and death that these are conditioned by the cognising consciousness – so how numerous are these defining activities (行相)?

434a05

Answer: There are five states or conditions of consciousness:[288] the *first* is consciousness of the direct, first, immediate [perception] (率爾心), explained as the initial encounter with an object (聞法創初); coming across it in the / as objective world, then it arises. The *second* is a searching, discursive consciousness: the world as object is not yet understood so there is just seeking / investigation (尋求). The *third* is the consciousness of conclusion, which appreciates (審知) the substance of the object (法體), so that a conclusion arises. The *fourth* is consciousness both defiled and pure in which the object is explained as both / either liking and / or disliking, thus the arising of defilement and purity. The *fifth* is consciousness of smooth progression (等流) [between cause and effect]: thought after thought is conditioned / programmed by [associated causes pertaining to (緣)] the object, so that before and after is a continuity. The *Essay on the Forest of Meanings in the Dharma Grove of the Great Vehicle* says,

As for discussing the five characteristics of consciousness, it is just like

---

[288] 五心 five states or conditions of consciousness produced by objective perception: 卒爾心 direct, immediate or instantaneous, the first impression; 尋求心 attention, or inquiry; 決定心 conclusion, decision; 染淨心 the effect, evil or good; 等流心 the production from other causations.

the visual-consciousness's (眼識) first alighting (初墮) upon an object, called 'the suddenly-alighting-upon-consciousness' (率爾墮心) – for in that first [spontaneous] instant, thought consciousness (意識) is not yet conditioned to (familiar with) this (the object); it arises with the present instance, also called 'sudden[ly].' As the *Yogâcārabhūmi-śāstra* declares, thought consciousness arises spontaneously disorientated when it's conditioning/programming is not familiar with the object (緣不串習境時) and no volition etc. arising. At this time thought-conscious perception is called 'the suddenly-alighting-upon-[an an unfamiliar object] consciousness'. The moment volition [欲] arises, it therefore seeks to classify and to assimilate [discursively] (等攝), also discussed in section [seventy-six] on wisdom-insight in the *Sutra on Understanding Profound and Esoteric Doctrine*.[289] The five consciousnesses (senses, 五識) certainly are distinctive, yet all arise at the same time. So the thinking consciousness (*mano-vijñāna* 意識), arises together with the others simultaneously; therefore seeing together with thinking is called 'the sudden consciousness' (率爾心) because it alights suddenly upon an object first (初卒墮境故).[290] Since this is the first response of perception (緣), it is not yet recognised whether the object is good or bad. In order to recognise [the object] therefore, it has, secondly, to seek it out and so here is synergy (a co-arising) with volition, due to the expectation/hope [in seeking to know] the object (希望境). After it has already been sought out, it discerns (識知) its object for the first time and therefore a conclusion arises, so that the object is understood as having been definitely determined [in its particularity].

The spheres of consciousness (識界) have become distinct: appropriated by correct reasoning (取正因), there is synergy [of reasoning] with various external appearances (相): so that [for example], in enmity abides the bad; in intimacy abides the good; in the middle abides indifference. Consciousness defiled and pure arises and from this defilement and purity, thought conscious (意識) being anterior, permeates (引生) visual consciousness, whose nature is both good and defiled. It arises in accordance with what has gone before. It is called the '[defiled and pure]-together-flowing-con-

---

[289] 解深密經及決擇論說 T676–9. (T1861.45.0256a06).
[290] The terminology is fluid – 率爾 and 初卒.

sciousness.' (等流心). Likewise as the visual consciousness arises, so it is also with the ear consciousness and the rest.[291]

An ancient worthy asked, 'The five states of consciousness within the eight consciousnesses[292] – how many states of consciousness are there in each?'

Answer: The first five consciousnesses have four states of consciousness, excepting the searching consciousness, because they lack [the capacity] to differentiate (無分別故). The sixth consciousness has five states of consciousness; the seventh lacks two states of consciousness, [namely] the suddenly alighting [perception] and the searching consciousness but possesses three states of consciousness: of conclusion/certainty,[293] of the defiled and pure and of 'together flowing'. The seventh is therefore referred to as constantly responding/conditioned to the present objective situation and lacks an instant alighting [perception].

Question: The seventh [consciousness, *manas*] manifests [continually] discursive conceptualisations (計度分別), so why is there no searching consciousness present?

Answer: The state of consciousness that does not yet search is completely reliant on/in accord with the 'instant-alighting' [perception on an unidentified

---

[291] 大乘法苑義林章 *Dasheng fayuan yilin zhang,* 'Essay on the Forest of Meanings in the Dharma Grove of the Great Vehicle.' by Kuiji 窺基 (632–682). T1861.45.0256a02. (T1579.30.0291b17)

[292] The eight consciousnesses: the five senses plus the sixth, *manovijñāna* 意識, the conceptualising region of consciousness thought; the seventh *manas* 末那識, assaying the relative benefit or harm to the self posed by external objects and situations; the eighth *ālayavijñāna* 阿賴耶識 is known as the base consciousness 本識, store consciousness 藏識, or seed consciousness 種子識, understood to be the actual subject of transformation. DDB.

[293] In the *Yogâcārabhūmi-śāstra,* (T1579) a condition of settling into thought that occurs in the process of perception, subsequent to the 'seeking consciousness' 尋求心.

object] – then later the searching consciousness arises. The seventh, as it lacks the instant-alighting state, searching is also not present.

Question: Since the first five [consciousnesses] have an 'instant-alighting' (率爾) [perception of an unidentified object], why is there no searching / investigating [state]?

Answer: The searching [consciousness needs to] have two conditions, which are parallel (方有). The first [**434b**] is that the 'instant-alighting' consciousness leads [to] the second state, namely, a discriminating thought (分別心). Although the first five kinds of [consciousnesses] possess an 'instant-alighting' [perception], still, there are no discursive conceptualisations. The eighth consciousness has three states of consciousness, [namely], 'instant-alighting' [perception], the state of certainty [regarding the object perceived] and the 'together-flowing' but it lacks consciousness of purity and impurity and the searching [consciousness].

Question: The eighth and the seventh [consciousnesses] constantly respond in concert to the present situation (object), so how could such [a state as an] 'instantly-alighting' [perception on an unidentified object] come about?

Answer: The seventh [consciousness] responds to (perceives) objects, which means, there is no interruption [in its activity]. The eighth responds to objects, [but] the objects experience interruptions. Therefore the eighth, from the moment of undergoing birth, initiates the causal conditions (創緣) in the three realms[294] and the three kinds of objects.[295]

Question: From the moment of undergoing birth, the seventh consciousness

---

[294] Desire, form and the formless realms; or, past, present and future.

[295] Three kinds of objects 三類境. In Yogācāra theory, objects of consciousness are divided into three categories. 性境 direct apprehension of an object in its own nature. 獨影境 arbitrarily imagined objects. 帶質境 A mixture of the first two, e. g., a memory.

115

also initiates the three realms, but why is there no 'instantly alighting' consciousness in the eighth consciousness?

434b07

Answer: The seventh [consciousness] complies with what is bound [to it by afflictions] and always conditions the current environment (當界) of / by / through the eighth consciousness. Here is an aid to understanding: the seventh consciousness is always internally conditioned by one object [at a time] and so there is no [state of] 'suddenly-alighting' [upon an unfamiliar object]. The eighth consciousness's external factors (外緣) are of many objects, therefore there is [the state of] 'suddenly-alighting' [upon a multiple of external objects of perception], but there is [yet] no differentiation, that is, there is no searching out / investigation [of an object's particularity].

434b10

Question: Within the five states of consciousness, which [states] perfumes (impregnates, suffuses) the seeds and which do not perfume the seeds?[296]

434b11

Answer: There are two explanations for the 'suddenly-alighting [upon an unfamiliar object] consciousness' (率爾心). The first says that because the naturally occurring (任運) perception of [external] objects does not [impinge] powerfully, it does not perfume the seeds. The second [explanation] says that, if conditioned perception gives rise to (alights upon?) an object [for the first time], then it does not perfume a seed. If, [on the other hand], conditioned perception already has knowledge of and familiarity (熟) with an object, then, because of the power of repeated cultivation / exposure, the seed [known and familiar] is [further] perfumed.

As for the other [of the five] states of consciousness, they are all [already] perfumed seeds. Here is the explanation: it is just as when 'suddenly alighting upon' the hearing of an object of sound; the event does not simply give rise to a

---

[296] In Yogācāra the seeds are one phase of the latent potentialities of all mental and physical dharmas which are stored in the eighth consciousness (*ālayavijñāna*). Coming into existence as the result of present activities and conditions, the seeds result either in actual effects, or in [creating] new potentialities [latent seeds], giving rise to continued existence. DDB.

familiarity with the object of the sound, but all (of the sound?) perfumes actual sound seeds, for there are a further nine states of consciousness to complete the cycle (輪) [that recognises the sound]. Expanded and abbreviated [explanations] are not the same [yet] the principle of reality is one and the same. This consciousness is like a wheel / circle [of different states], changing by following objects. Therefore a sutra says that the body is not the turner of thought (身非念輪)[297] but 'following thought it changes.' (隨念而轉)[298] What does this mean?

> The Theravada masters[299] established the 'nine cycles of consciousness' (九心輪): one, there are distinctions [of states, conditions, objects]; two, a capacity emerges to impel / stimulate; three, seeing / insight; four, searching; five, penetration; six, to establish provisionally; seven, potent power; eight, conditions for returning; nine, there is a distinction in essence.

As when first coming to birth, yet unable to differentiate, consciousness is only a spontaneous arising in which conditions are in the objects coming up, called 'there are distinctions' [of state, conditions, objects]. If there is an event / object arising / occurring, consciousness then wishes to perceive / take part in it, in which case alert awareness (警覺) arises, called 'a capacity to stimulate (引發) [perception]. Since this consciousness has made an upward turn [in perception] to this object, it sees clearly and looks at it carefully. Having seen it, it then turns into (成) [the state of] discursive inquiry. Examining [whether it is] good or bad and having examined it, then with a penetrating consciousness it [knows it to be] good or bad and so provisionally establishes the [activity of the] consciousness. There arises then a verbalisation of biased subjectivity (分別) pronouncing it good or bad. According to [its biased subjectivity of] whether the object is good or bad, there is an impetus towards action (動作勢用). Since activity has been generated, there is a desire [to gain the object, therefore to] abandon (休廢) the Way – hence returning to the conditioned [subjective perception] formerly prevailing. Having turned back to this conditioning is also to return to a state of discrimination (還歸有分). The naturally occurring perception of objects is called the ninth [state of] consciousness. It can take on the explanations of a cycle (輪), in which the seeing consciousness passes through

---

[297] Also in fasc. 3, T48.0432a21.

[298] T0721.17.0248b24.

[299] The following passage is taken from T1831.43.0635b18-c06 by Kuiji.

the six consciousnesses. The remainder are [also] just consciousness, possessing discriminatory states of consciousness passing through birth and death: reverting to a consciousness condition that only attains death.

If someone is free of desire, then death is merely of the discriminating consciousness, for since there is no craving for self, there is nothing that reverts to perceiving objects (緣), nor [anything] giving rise to yearnings. [**434c**] Those not yet free of desire, by reverting to a consciousness of perceiving objects, suffer death, because of the yearning. If an object is encountered, then consciousness is activated. If there is no aberrant [perception] of objects (異境), there is the ever-abiding aspect of the whole (有分), a spontaneously arising continuum (相續). Thus, seeing by inquiry before and after is indeterminate (not fixed).

434c03

Question: By following a biased subjectivity (分別), a true and a deluded consciousness are set up; in general, how many kinds of these two consciousnesses are there?

434c04

Answer: The *Mahāprajñāpāramitāśāstra* says that there are two kinds of Ways.[300] The first Way is absolute emptiness. The second Way discriminates between good and bad. If the Way of absolute emptiness has still not reached the One, could there be talk of many [ones]? If the Way is discriminating between good or bad, then the interpretation of principle would depend on discrimination (理從義別), as with the matter of the [innumerable] grains of sand in the River Ganges, yet it is simply about the one consciousness.

There are four interpretations of old:[301] one is 'hṛdaya' (*xin*), this is called the physical heart. Within the body are the five viscera (heart, lungs, liver, kidneys and spleen or stomach) as clarified in the *Yellow Court Classic*.[302] The second

---

[300] But Yanshou is only citing, not quoting from the 大智度論, T1509.25.0085a15.

[301] Of the four kinds of 'consciousness', as used in Zongmi's 宗密 Chan Chart 禪源諸詮集都序 (T 2015.48.401c23): (1) physical consciousness 肉團心 (Skt. *hṛdaya*), (2) consciousness considering perceived objects 緣慮心, (3) the collectively arising consciousness 集起心 (also 質多心; eighth consciousness 第八識), and (4) intrinsic consciousness 堅實心 (also 乾栗馱心; thusness consciousness 眞如心).

[302] 黃廷經 A Daoist meditation (visualisation) text of the Shangqing 上清 (Supreme Purity) lineage received by Lady Wei Huacun 魏華存 (252–334 CE) from an unknown source in 288CE.

is consciousness thinking and self-differentiating objects (緣慮自分境) – these
are the eight consciousnesses because all can think about various subject and
object realms; [for example] colour is the object of visual consciousness. There
are the [six] bodily senses and the seed potentialities of the container realm
(種子器世界) – the realm of the store-consciousness (*ālayavijñāna*). Each is
conditioned by a part, therefore they are called 'self-differentiating (自分). The
third is *citta* (質多耶), this is called 'collectively arising consciousness' (集起
心), [since] only the eighth consciousness accumulates seeds [of potentiality],
giving rise to actions in the present. The fourth, *hṛdaya* (乾栗陀耶 heart, mind,
core), this is called intrinsic consciousness (堅實心), also called the true innate
consciousness (貞實心) – this is the thusness of consciousness. Therefore, the
eighth consciousness is not differentiated into a [separate] self-essence (無別自
體). It is simply the thusness of consciousness, but because it is not perceived,
it is mixed with a multitude of deluded concepts. The meaning is that there is
a blending and a not blending. The meaning of blending: it can contain impurity and purity, regarded as the store consciousness (*tathāgatagharba*). As for
not blending, the essence is ever unchanging, regarded as thusness – all is the
tathāgatagharba. Therefore the *Laṅkāvatāra-Sūtra* says,

> As for peaceful cessation, [its] name is the one consciousness
> As for the one consciousness, it is precisely the
> *tathāgatagharba*[303]

The *tathāgatagharba* is also in bondage to the Dharma-body. A sutra says,

> Hidden as the *tathāgatagharba*, manifest as the Dharma-body[304]

Therefore known as the four states of consciousness; originally of the same,
one essence, only from factors of delusion and awakening it becomes many. A
gatha from a sutra says,

> Buddha discourses on the *tathāgatagharba*
> Taking it as the *ālaya* (store)

---

[303] T0671.16.0519a01.

[304] 大乘起信論義疏 *Dacheng qiconsciousness lun yishu*, 'Commentary on the Awakening of Faith' attributed to (?) Huiyuan 慧遠 (523–592) of Jingying. T1843.44.0183b18.

Impaired discernment (惡慧) cannot know it
The store is precisely the store-house consciousness[305]

Concerning Buddha discoursing on the *tathāgatagharba*, it is really the name of the Dharma-body in bondage; taking it as the *ālaya* is precisely the store-[house] consciousness. Impaired discernment cannot know it – the store is precisely the *ālaya* consciousness. There are those who aver that the essences of thusness and of the *ālaya* are distinct – this is impaired discernment. Now, although the four states of consciousness are of the same essence, the meaning of true and false is distinct. There is also a difference between the root and the branches. The first three [of the four states] are characteristics; the last is the [true] nature. The [true] nature and characteristics [work together] without obstructions; all are of the one consciousness, which means that the fourth, true consciousness (真心) serves as the cardinal meaning (宗旨). Furthermore, as an ancient worthy explained in detail concerning the one consciousness, one should regard the one consciousness of the *tathāgatagharba* as containing two meanings.

The first meaning, simply, is to be done with (絕) characteristics [in favour of] essence (or essence having done with characteristics 體絕相), which is the gate to thusness; the sense being that it (the essence) is neither defiled nor pure, neither coming to be nor ceasing to be. It neither moves nor transforms, being even and equal, of one flavour. There are no distinctions in the [true] nature, for all living beings are [**435a**] nirvana, they do not require (不待) cessation. Mortals and Maitreya are of the same realm (mundane and nirvana).

The second meaning is that to follow the arising and cessation of phenomena is the aspect of [their] birth and death, referred to as submitting to the suffusion of shifting movements turning into defilements and purity. Although defilements and purity take shape, the [true] nature is ever immovable. Only from the immovable are defilements and purity able to take shape, which is therefore immovable, whilst also an aspect of the movable. The *Laṅkāvatāra-Sūtra* says,

The *tathāgatagharba* is called the *ālayavijñāna*, but nescience is shared

---

[305] 大乘密嚴經 *Dacheng miyan jing, Ghanavyūha sutra,* 'Great Vehicle Sutra of [the Pure Land], Densely Adorned, translated by Divākara 地婆訶羅 (613–687). To681.16.0747a17.

with the seven consciousnesses – like great ocean waves are never separate [from each other].[306]

It is also said,

> Concerning the *tathāgatagharba*, it is suffused, from beginningless time, with conceptual proliferations (虛偽) and unwholesome habits, called the store of consciousness (識藏 i. e., *ālayavijñāna*).[307]

If those who [comply with] this one consciousness by deducing that the branches return to the root, they are referred to as verifying the primary meaning and then come to liberation. The primary meaning concerns the nature of phenomena. When insight is gained into the nature of phenomena there is then a release from the bonds of phenomena. The *Huayan Sūtra* says,

> Everything is created by the one consciousness. [Chengguan's] commentary says, concerning just this one consciousness, that everything in the three realms comes forth from only consciousness (唯心).[308] All the teachings lead to validating only consciousness. What then is the one consciousness that creates the three realms? There are three [meanings]:[309] the first [concerns the adherents of] the two vehicles (*sravakas* and *pratyekabuddhas*), referred to as 'there are objects in front of one,' which are not understood to be [produced by] only consciousness. Even on hearing about the one consciousness, it is merely regarded as one of the ultimate truths (真諦). Some say that it is due to the 'manifestations of consciousness' (心轉變) but that not everything is 'consciousness'.
>
> The second meaning is about the ripening [of of the latent power of good and unwholesome activities / seeds] in the *ālayavijñāna* – called the one consciousness. There are simply no external objects, therefore it is said that it is the one consciousness.
>
> The third meaning is the nature of the *tathāgatagharba*'s purity – the one

---

[306] T0671.16.0556c01.

[307] T0670.16.0510b07.

[308] 唯心 *wei xin,* only consciousness: in the 'Awakening of Faith' and *Huayan* it is a different formulation from 'Only-Consciousness' 唯識 *wei shi* of the Yogācāra school.

[309] T1735.35.0806b20 (略有三義).

consciousness. Principle is not constituted of two essences, so it is called the one consciousness.[310]

It should be known that the two dharmas of worldling and sage and the two gates of defilement and purity are nothing but the one consciousness. Furthermore, this one consciousness, briefly, is the [true] nature and [its] characteristics, essence and function, root and branches, which are the entrance to the universal equality (等義) [of the one consciousness].

What is more, there are ten explanations / approaches;[311] the first [one] is the nominal explanation of the one consciousness; so then the followers of the two vehicles refer to reality as having external dharmas, simply because consciousness is changeable, so it is called the 'one consciousness.' (故說 一心) The next nine entrances are about the reality of only one consciousness.

The second [entrance / approach] is to perceive (相見) all as existent, therefore said to be the one consciousness – these eight consciousnesses taken all together with the various functions of consciousness and their changeable objective aspects. Unprocessed raw perceptive input and the objective aspect of the projected image are complete,[312] due to the power of permeation to the link of becoming (有支) and the rest [of the twelve linked chain of causation] that the three realms of transformation [serve as the basis for] circumstantial and direct retribution and so forth (依正等報).

The third [approach] is to subsume characteristics and return to insight,

---

[310] T1735.35.0806b17.

[311] 廣開有十 T1735.35.0806b28.

[312] 本影 Perception before thinking / re-cognition / interpretation (本) and after recognition / thinking / interpretation (影), i.e., the original and its shadow 本影; short for 本質, 'unprocessed, raw perceptive input-objective aspect' and 影像 'projected image-objective aspect.' These two aspects taken together are understood to constitute the 'objective aspect' 相分 of consciousness, Muller, DDB. For 影像 and 本質 see John P. Keenan's translation of the *Saṃdhinirmocana-Sūtra,* ch.VI, (T0676.16.0697c14). Also Charles Muller, 'Woncheuk 圓測 on Bimba 本質 and Pratibimba 影像 in his 'Commentary on the Saṃdhinirmocana-Sūtra' in *Journal of Indian and Buddhist Studies* Vol. 59, No.3, March 2011.

therefore explained as the one consciousness, also understood as the sovereign [consciousness as a whole] and its various factors (王數). Only that which transforms the objective aspect (相分) [the inner image evoked by cognition], being without other forms of arising (無別種生), is capable of insight into the arising of consciousness (識生) and of containing those shadow [images] emerging (帶彼影起).

The fourth [approach] is to subsume the various factors [of consciousness] (攝數) and return to the sovereign [consciousness as a whole] (歸王), thus called the one consciousness, only common to the eight consciousnesses, because those mental factors [concomitant with consciousness] (心所) rely upon the sovereign [consciousness] which is without essence/substance [but] also [manifests] mental transformations (心變).[313]

The explanation: concerning 'subsuming characteristics/factors to return to insight.' A gatha in the *Weishi Lun* says,

> 'Only Consciousness' (唯識) is without an objective realm
> Because its perception is without defilements and delusion
>
> If people have cataracts [in their eyes]
> They will see such things as hairs and moons[314]

Now whenever a treatise is composed, it contains three explanations: the first is to establish the meaning, which is the initial [group of] phrases; the second is to induce realisation, which is the second [group of] phrases; the third concerns metaphor, which is under two [groups of] phrases. The *Guan Suoyuanyuan lun* says,

> Inner consciousness (內識) seems like external manifestations
> It is consciousness perceiving [itself] as [external] objects
> Given that these characteristics are in consciousness
> They then empower consciousness to arise[315]

---

[313] T1735.35.0806b28- c08.

[314] T1588.31.0063c27.

[315] 觀所緣緣論 *Guan suoyuanyuan lun*, 'Treatise on Contemplating Objective Condi-

The meaning is that [**435b**] inner consciousness produces a similitude [of itself manifesting] as external object, perceived as objective perception. Given that the visual and the other consciousnesses carry (contain 帶) those arising characteristics / factors, it is from those therefore that consciousness is born.

The conclusion: the various consciousnesses are exclusively internal objects; the characteristics / forms are perceived as [external] objects; the principle is fully established' (理極成也). So it is not that there is a complete lack of forms / characteristics, for characteristics belong wholly to consciousness, which is why it is called returning to insight.[316]

Concerning 'to subsume the various factors (攝數) [of consciousness] and return to the sovereign [consciousness]' (攝數歸王), as a gatha in the *Treatise on the Scripture of Adorning the Great Vehicle* says,

> The realm of self and the two manifestations / appearances (二光)
> Afflictions all arise in common with delusion
> Such are all these discriminations
> The two realities should be kept apart[317]

(T1736 continues) Meaning: the realm of self (自界) refers to the self of the *ālaya*-consciousness seeds; the two manifestations (二光) refers to the ability [of the subject] to grasp the manifestations (取光) and the manifestations that are grasped; these are equally discriminatory (delusive). Because of the combination of ignorance with all the other afflictions these [two] therefore arise. All the discriminations are like this. The two facts should be kept apart. The two facts refer to the fact of grasping and to the ability [of the subject] to grasp – these two factual defilements should be sought / are required to be kept apart.[318] Thus a gatha in the treatise says,

tions' by Dignāga 陳那, translated by Xuanzang in 657. T1624.31.0888c17.

[316] T1736.36.0526c04.

[317] T1736.36.0526c11 quoting T1604.31.0613a17.

[318] 大乘莊嚴經論 *Dasheng zhuangyanjing lun (Mahāyāna-sūtrâlaṃkāra)*, 'Treatise on the Scripture of Adorning the Great Vehicle' attributed to Asaṅga 無著 (4ᵗʰ cent.) translated by Prabhākaramitra 波羅頗蜜多羅 CE 630−33. T1604.31.0613a16.

The ability to grasp and that which is grasped
These two are manifestations (光) of only consciousness (唯心)
The manifestations of craving and belief/conviction
These two manifestations are not two things (法 dharmas)

The explanation is that persons investigating 'only [projections of] consciousness' should get to know that the ability to grasp [and] that which is grasped – these two kinds are only manifestations (emanations of) consciousness.[319]

[The *Zhuangyan lun* says:][320] The fifth [approach] is to return to the root by means of the branches, called the one (universal) consciousness, meaning that the [first] seven [transforming] consciousnesses are all different functions (功能) of the root (*ālayavijñāna*) consciousness since they have no distinct essences (無別體故). A gatha to the [*Lengjia*] sutra also says,

The example is a mighty ocean wave
It does not possess a definite number of marks[321]
All cognising consciousnesses (識心) are like this
[Their] diversity too cannot be obtained

The sixth [approach] is to subsume the characteristics and return to the [true] nature, called the one consciousness, meaning that these eight consciousnesses are all without intrinsic self-essences. There is only the *tathāgatagharba* manifesting even and equally. Other marks (characteristics) all disappear (盡). [A sutra] says, 'All sentient beings have just the aspect (相) of nirvana.'[322] [the *Lengjia* says], 'The indestructible characteristics are eight (or do not neglect the eight characteristics 不壞相有八), [323] the absence of characteristics is also not a characteristic.'

The seventh [approach], [the true] nature and characteristics (noumenon

---

319 T1604.31.0613b12.
320 T1735 supposedly quoting T1604.
321 大方廣佛華嚴經 T009.0278.0787b19: 猶如虛空性　無有若干相.
322 T1736.36.0461c18.
323 T1735.35.0806c17.

and phenomena 性相) interpenetrate, called the one consciousness, meaning the *tathāgatagharba*. Wholly in accord with the phenomena [of conditioned arising], all undertakings are accomplished out of one's own / intrinsic nature. The origin is not subject to arising and cessation, it is principle and phenomena blended without obstructions. It is therefore the two truths of the one consciousness, all without obstructions.

The eighth [approach] is the entry into the interpenetration of phenomena, called the one consciousness, meaning that due to / from the [true] nature of consciousness interpenetration is perfect and without obstructions because the [true] nature creates (以性成事) the phenomena. Phenomena too merge with each other without obstruction – one entered, all [entered]. Within each of the motes of dust the realm of Dharma is seen. Devas, men and asuras are not absent from a single mote.

The ninth [approach], all phenomena are identical in non-difference (相即), called the one consciousness, meaning that the reliance of phenomena is on the [true] nature. There are no phenomena separate [from this reliance of] phenomena [on the true nature] (事無別事) since there is no difference between each other; the nature of consciousness and phenomena too are all just one (the same); the one, many and the many, one and the same (事亦一切即一, 一即是多, 多即一等).

The tenth [approach], Indra's net,[324] is without obstructions, called the one consciousness, meaning all is [reflected] within one [vertex] and within [each of vertices] these all again are all [reflected], without end (endlessly interdependent), all by means of consciousness (心識) of the *tathāgatagharba* nature; perfect interpenetration without end, due to the nature of thusness, therefore ultimately inexhaustible.[325]

[324] 帝網 *Di wang*. A vast net hangs in Indra's palace, in which a multifaceted jewel at each vertex reflects all the jewels at all the other vertices. The image of Indra's net is used to describe the interconnectedness or perfect interfusion (*yuan rong* 圓融) of all phenomena in the universe, the absolute in the relative, the relative in the absolute. All things are of the same fundamental nature, all are thusness, and thusness is all.

[325] T1735.35.0806c09.

Contemplating all dharmas as thusness, in all times and places, all is due to Indra's net, as the *Whirlpool* gatha says,

> If one has an urge [435c] for awareness of the true emptiness principle
> The thusness within the body is also present everywhere outside
> Delusion and non-delusion are equal, of one essence
> The realm of the true Dharma is everywhere the same
> Not separated from illusory forms yet perceiving emptiness
> This is precisely thusness, containing all things
> One thought can illumine entry into many aeons
> Each thought through the aeons contains every other
> Within one realm is the knowledge of everything
> Within one moment of knowledge (一智) are all realms
> Merely adopting one thought-moment is insight into all realms
> Each and every realm is merged in one time
> Time and place, Indra's net manifests, multi-faceted
> All is supra-normal consciousness (智通) without obstructions[326]

Concerning whirlpools, they are the places where eddies and undercurrents of water go; firstly therefore, [being whirlpools], they are very deep; secondly, on account of turning this way and that, they are therefore, thirdly, difficult to ferry across. The ocean of Dharma swirls like this too; firstly therefore, only a Buddha can fathom [its depths]; secondly, the true and the untrue are mutually accommodating (circle round each other) and therefore it is difficult to fathom the beginning [of one] and the end of [the other]; and thirdly, due to hearing of emptiness designated as emptiness, hearing of being designated as being, then [people] sink into a whirlpool [of confusion]. If this teaching (宗) be not understood, difficult it would be to transcend the ocean of existence. Following the waves of good and bad, drifting islets of sufferings and happiness, a compassionate vessel [of rescue] is not met with. How could they climb up the shore of awakening? As the gatha says,

> Thusness is the pure realm of Dharma
> The one has never ceased to exist

---

[326] 漩澓[偈] *Xuanfu* [*ji*] by Dharma master Dushun (557–640) 杜順法師, first patriarch of the *Huayan* lineage. F28.1083.0627b05 (slightly different).

In obeying the conditions of defilement and purity
It thereupon becomes the ten realms of dharma[327]

Obeying the conditions of defilement becomes the six worldly [of the ten] dharma realms; obeying the conditions of purity becomes the [last] four sacred realms of dharma.

The six worldly realms of dharma: first is the dharma realm of the devas; second is the human dharma realm; third, the dharma realm of the asuras; fourth is the dharma realm of the hells; fifth is the dharma realm of the hungry ghosts; sixth, the dharma realm of the animals.

The four sacred dharma realms: the first is the dharma realm of the *sravaka* (hearer); the second, that of the *pratyekabuddha*; third is the dharma ream of a *bodhisattva*; the fourth, the dharma realm of a Buddha. Living beings, as the above [first six of the ten dharma realms], are of the true nature but due to differences in feeling and thinking, they then rise and fall into the six destinies. All the sages are in the dharma [realm] of *wuwei* (unpremeditated action) because the actions of wisdom are of a different order, so that the last four sacred [realms of the ten dharma realms] are the highest [realms]. Nevertheless, although the traces of worldlings and sages rise and fall, fetters and liberation seem to be different; [yet] within the realm of the one true Dharma change is originally non-existent. Also, according to the *Huayan* School,[328] the one consciousness obeys principle and phenomena (absolute and relative). It establishes four kinds of dharma realms.

Concerning the first dharma realm of principle [according to the *Huayan* School], the meaning is that it is the realm / continuum of the [true] nature, a realm of inexhaustible dharma-phenomena [since] everything [there] is of the same nature (一理法界者, 界是性義, 無盡事法, 同一性故).

As to the second dharma realm of phenomena, the realm is [occupied by] separate objects (義); [yet] each object [although] it exists separately, has aspects that harmonise.

---

[327] Source unknown. The ten realms of Dharma, in Tiantai these are the realms of hell denizens, hungry ghosts, animals, asuras, humans, gods; *śrāvaka*s, pratyekabuddhas, bodhisattvas and Buddhas.

[328] From 註華嚴法界觀門 *Zhu Huayan fajie guanmen*, 'Elucidations on the contemplation of the Huayan Dharma Realm' by Zongmi 宗密 (Guifeng 圭峰 780–841). T1884.45.0684b25.

Concerning the third dharma realm of principle and phenomena, there is no obstruction [between them]. The [true] nature and objects all blend completely without obstructions.

Concerning the fourth dharma realm, phenomena [interpenetrating] phenomena without obstructions, all aspects of phenomenal dharmas harmonise; each one according to [the true] nature interpenetrates without limit.

By means of these ten dharma realms and due to the four dharma realms of principle and phenomena (ocean and waves), the [true] nature and characteristics (phenomena) are thus engaged in (entered). The real and the conventional (真俗) interpenetrate and emerge far and wide (遍出), inexhaustibly creating all kinds of dharma realms without limit. Nevertheless, it is the complete dharma realm of the one consciousness. The wholly complete realm of dharma's one consciousness accords with [both] the powerful and the powerless (*or*, active and the passive? 隨有力無力) – it establishes the one, establishes the many, since they are mutually supportive, mutually interpenetrating, sometimes hidden, sometimes revealed. [**436a**] It is like integral emptiness (一空), everywhere all things and formative images (像) are connected. It is like one [body] of water gathering up myriad great billowing waves. To enter into the Ancestral Mirror (入宗鏡中) [teachings, the waves] appear calmed; there is also a place to enter that can be entered. The two types of dharma realm, as Qingliang [Chengguan]'s commentary states,

> Begin by clarifying the place of entry. Generally, there is only one truly unimpeded dharma realm. To discuss its nature and characteristics does not go beyond phenomena and principle, in accord with its distinctions in meaning.
>
> In brief, there are five entrances [to the realm of reality, *dharma dhātu*]:[329] the *first* is the phenomenal (conditioned) dharma realm; the *second* is the noumenal (unconditioned) dharma realm; the *third*, the realm of both phenomenal and noumenal; the *fourth*, the realm of neither phenomenal nor noumenal; the *fifth* is the unimpeded dharma realm, the unity of the phenomenal and noumenal.
>
> However, the five [entrances to the dharma realm of reality, *dharma dhātu*] each have two aspects. As to the *first* [entrance] to the phenomenal

---

[329] 五種法界 The Huayan school's five forms / aspects of *dharma dhātu* (realm of reality). DCBT: 124.

[有為 dharma realm], it concerns the <u>first</u> of the two [aspects門], the root consciousness (本識 *ālayavijñāna*) that can support all seeds (法種子) and its name is the dharma realm. As a treatise says, 'A realm from the beginningless beginning, etc.' – this is in agreement with the meaning of the basis (因) and essence of this realm; it is not restricted to the Dharma body (*dharmakāya*).

[Concerning] the <u>second</u> [of the two aspects to the entrance of the phenomenal dharma realm], the dharmas of the three time periods have distinct boundaries, called dharma realm, as the chapter on the Inconceivable Meaning [不思議品] says, 'All the Buddhas know that absolutely nothing remains of any dharma realm of the past,'[330] etc. – this then is the meaning of the separate [yet] harmonising (分劑).

The *second* entrance [of the five entrances to the dharma realm of reality, *dharma dhātu*] concerns the two [aspects] of the noumenal dharma realm (無為法界). The <u>first</u> [aspect] is the [original] purity of the [true/self] nature (性淨), because [even] at the worldly stage, the [true] nature is ever pure, of the one quality of true emptiness, since dharmas know no distinctions [between pure and impure].

The <u>second</u> [aspect to the noumenal dharma realm], freedom from defilements, so called from the antidote/cure, since the purity is then revealed, according to the shallowness or depth of practice, is therefore divided into ten kinds.

The *third* [of the five entrances to the dharma realm of reality, *dharma dhātu*] concerns the two [aspects] to both the phenomenal and noumenal dharma realm. The <u>first</u> aspect [of the two] accords with the characteristics, referred to as the aggregate of sensation, thinking, volition, the five colours (forms, objects of the senses) and the eight noumenon:[331] these are the sixteen dharmas, only known by consciousness, within the eighteen compositional elements of cognition (of the objective world十八界),[332] the name is the dharma realm.

---

[330] T0278.09.0597c13 quoted in T1735.

[331] 善法真如, 不善法真如, 無記法真如, 虛空, 非擇滅, 擇滅, 不動, 想受滅. Thusness of wholesome dharmas; thusness of unwholesome dharmas; emptiness; non-analytical cessation; analytical cessation; the immovable; cessation of feeling and perception.

[332] I.e., the six sense faculties, their objects and the six consciousnesses belonging to these faculties.

The <u>second</u> aspect [to both the phenomenal and noumenal dharma realm], unimpeded, refers to the dharma realm of the one consciousness; it contains two parts. The first is consciousness in its aspect of thusness; the second is the aspect of the arising and ceasing of consciousness. Although these two parts comprehensively include all the various dharmas, nevertheless, these two never mix with each other (不相雜 remain unadulterated). This would be as if [deep] water [giving rise] to waves were not still, as if gathering waves were not to move. Therefore the chapter on the transfer of merit ways (迴向品/第四迴向),[333] 'In the phenomenal realm the noumenal is revealed, yet the characteristics (marks) of the phenomenal [realm] are not annihilated. In the noumenal realm the phenomenal dharmas are revealed, yet are not distinguished from the [true] nature of the noumenal.' This clarifies the non-obstruction between phenomena and principle.

The *fourth* [of the five entrances to the dharma realm of reality, *dharma dhātu*] concerns the two aspects of the dharma realm of neither phenomenal nor noumenal. The <u>first</u> aspect is the snatching away of the forms [of both principle and phenomena 形奪],[334] referred to as: conditions are not conditions devoid of principle, therefore it is not phenomenal (not conditioned 非有為). [Equally], principle is not principle devoid of conditions, therefore, it is not noumenal. The essence of Dharma is even and equal, [both] forms are snatched away and extinguished. The *Mahāprajñāparamītā-Sūtra* says,

Subhuti asked the Buddha, 'This Dharma is even and equal – is it conditioned or is it unconditioned?' The Buddha replied, 'It is neither conditioned nor is it unconditioned. Why? The unconditioned Dharma would not be able to be obtained without (apart from) the conditioned dharmas; the conditioned dharmas would not be able to be obtained apart from unconditioned Dharma. Sub-

[333] There are ten dedications: 十迴向 1) dedication to saving all beings without any mental image of sentient beings; 2) indestructible dedication; 3) dedication equal to all Buddhas; 4) dedication reaching all places; 5) dedication of inexhaustible treasuries of merit; 6) dedication causing all wholesome roots to endure; 7) dedication equally adapting to all sentient beings; 8) dedication with the character of thusness; 9) unbound liberated dedication; 10) Unfathomability of the *dharma dhātu*, also called Boundless dedication equal to the cosmos.

[334] 止觀十門 Ten approaches to cessation and analytical meditation: the fourth being 四理事形奪而俱盡, 故止觀兩亡而絕寄 T2016.48.0623b09.

huti, these are the conditioned dharmas (性=法) and the unconditioned Dharma; these two dharmas do not merge [yet] do not separate (不合不散).'335

> This is the explanation.336 The <u>second</u> of the two aspects [of the dharma realm of neither phenomenal nor noumenal] is non-reliance (無寄).337 This dharma realm is referred to as free of characteristics and free of the [true] nature, **[436b]** therefore it is not these two. Neither is it the two truths (二諦)338 nor are the two therefore reachable by names and words, because both are free/apart from [names and words]. As the *Sutra of the Explication of the Underlying Meaning* says,

Concerning all dharmas, they are, in short, of two kinds, referred to as conditioned [dharmas] and unconditioned ones. Within the conditioned ones there are neither conditioned nor unconditioned [dharmas]. The unconditioned is neither unconditioned nor conditioned, and so on.339

> The *fifth* [of the five entrances to the dharma realm of reality, *dharma dhātu*] concerns the two aspects of the unimpeded dharma realm, [the unity of the phenomenal and noumenal]. The <u>first</u> aspect is universal inclusion (普攝), referring to the four [double] aspects above, because all is subsumed into the one, therefore it is good fortune, whether beholding mountains and sea or seeing temple halls and shrines; everything bears the name of entering the dharma realm.
>
> The <u>second</u> aspect [of the unimpeded dharma realm] is perfect interpenetration, because it refers to principle fused with phenomena, causing phe-

---

335 T1735 quoting from T0220.07.0425a28 大般若波羅蜜多經 and from T0223.08.0415b16 摩訶般若波羅蜜經etc.

336 Back to T1735.35. 0908b14.

337 An approach, typically associated with Chan Buddhism, of seeing all things as absolutely empty, and thus there is nothing to be relied upon. Muller, DDB.

338 The ultimate truth 眞諦 (*paramârtha-satya*) and conventional truth 世俗諦 (*saṃvṛti-satya*).

339 解深密經 *Jie shenmi jing*, 'Sutra on Understanding Profound and Esoteric Doctrine' or 'Sutra of the Explication of the Underlying Meaning' translated by Xuanzang, 647 CE. 'The single most important scriptural source for the doctrines of the Yogācāra school' (DDB), translated into English by Keenan, John P. *The Scripture on Explanation of the Underlying Meaning*. T0676.16.0688c23.

nomena to harmonise without division (無分劑). A particle of dust is not small – it can contain the ten [Buddhist] realms.[340] The realm of the ocean is not large; it can covertly enter a particle of dust. Because phenomena reveal principle, it causes principle not to be without distinguishing [marks] (非無分), referred to as the one and the many are without obstruction (unimpeded). Sometimes it is called one dharma realm, sometimes, many dharma realms; thus, on account of one not being one, it is then many; many, not being many, is therefore one – and so up to multiples without end. That is why it is good fortune to temporarily hold hands, then, passing through many aeons, only now to enter the tall palace pavilion, gaining a universal view without limit, all of such types.

The above, being the five entrances [to the realm of reality, *dharma dhātu*] and their ten interpretations (義) (aspects), generally clarify the region entered – the dharma realm, which should fuse with the six characteristics of conditioned phenomena.[341]

The second clarification (see Qingliang [Chengguan]'s first clarification/commentary above) [concerns] the potential (能) to enter [the realm of reality, *dharma dhātu*] which is also through five means (門). The first is [through] pure faith; the second, by correct understanding/liberation; the third by cultivating practice; the fourth is through realisation consummated; the fifth through completion.

These five [means] of entry into the dharma realm just mentioned, have their two aspects (門). There is the potential to enter all five one by one. Following on the first that is entered then all five are potentially entered.

Second, these five [means] are potentially entered, such that they each enter every aspect sequentially. These two meanings of consciousness and its objects [as stated] above (*or,* these higher [functions of] consciousness

---

[340] The ten realms are, in ascending order of the degree of free will, compassion and happiness one feels, the worlds of: (1) hell, (2) hungry spirits, (3) animals, (4) asuras, (5) human beings (6) heavenly beings, (7) voice-hearers, (8) cause-awakened ones, (9) bodhisattvas, and (10) Buddhas.

[341] A set of concepts originating in the *DaśabhūmikaSūtra* of the *Dilun* 地論 school, later utilised by Huayan exegetes such as Fazang. These are: totality 總相, distinction 別相, sameness 同相, difference 異相, formation 成相, and disintegration 壞相. In Huayan philosophy these are considered to be interpenetrated 六相圓融. Muller/Lusthaus, DDB.

and its objects), and the ten interpretations/aspects and the six characteristics of conditioned phenomena perfectly interpenetrate; all integrate as a group, unimpeded in the dharma realm. [342]

As it is said in *The Hundred Gates to the Ocean of Meanings,*

> As for/those entering the dharma realm, meaning, afflicted conditioning [of the six sense fields] (塵緣) arises as dharmas and the dharmas accord with the manifestation of awareness (智顯); functions [though] possess distinctions as the bases of perception (界). These dharmas, because they have no [self] nature, possess no distinctions (無分劑), blending without the characteristics of duality, the same as thusness (真際) and emptiness and so on pervading all everywhere. Revealed in all situations, there is nothing that is not clear. Nevertheless, these isolated particles of dust [afflictions], together with all dharmas, do not see each other, nor know each other. Why? Since all is a wholly complete realm of Dharma, universally subsuming all things, there is, furthermore, absolutely no other Dharma subject to awakened insight (知見). A sutra says that just the Dharma realm is without a Dharma realm; the Dharma realm does not know a Dharma realm.[343]

If this is so, then even concerning there being no separate dharmas subject to awakened insight, why call it entry? It is due to the awakened situation that it is designated as entry, yet, even though there is entry, there is no place of entry. Were there a place to enter, then the meaning of the [true] nature of the emptiness of all dharmas would be mistaken, since the absence of a [true] nature and principle is identical (以無性理同故), so that every situation is an entry into the Dharma realm. Previously, concerning the ten [436c] dharma realms formed by the emotions and understanding of ordinary persons, who saw conditioned existence with [a mixture of] purity and the defilements, that is what constituted their mistake. Now, the entrance to Dharma arising from the [true] nature, and in accord [with the teaching of] the Huayan [sutra], all becomes the

---

[342] T1735.35.0908a16.

[343] 華嚴經義海百門 *Huayanjing yihai bomen,* 'The Hundred Gates to the Ocean of Meanings (Samādhis) of the Avatamsaka Sutra' by Fazang 法藏 (643–712). T1875.45.0627b16.

134

Dharma realm of thusness. Whether coming to be or ceasing to be, whether defiled or pure, all has become the realm of Dharma. A sutra says,

> Those who distinguish all the forms of the countless characteristics of disintegration are called superior in wisdom. An ancient commentator explains that the forms of the six destinies, destruction/ceasing of the good, destruction of meditation; the form of the two vehicles, destruction of cause, destruction of effect; the form of the bodhisattvas, the destruction of existence, destruction of non-existence. So too for the form of the Buddhas, the destruction of all the above destructions; the realm of Dharma as destroyer; neither destruction nor non-destruction – all is the realm of Dharma.[344]

436c07

Question: Consciousness is designated by four names, revealing ten interpretations; exactly how many meanings are there to these names of consciousness? (識)

Answer: If the standpoint is from the common aspects of intrinsic attributes (同門自相), there is no difference. If the standpoint is the different aspects of general attributes (異門共相), [then] allowing for the interpretations that are seemingly various designations, there are nine interpretations in terms of the noumenal and phenomenal (性相). There are five interpretations comprising inner and outer. Concerning the designations which are nine: the first is visual consciousness; the second, auditory consciousness; the third, olfactory consciousness; the fourth, gustatory consciousness; the fifth, tactile (body) consciousness; the sixth, conscious mental/conceptualising consciousness (*mano-vijñāna*); the seventh, sub-conscious organ of thought (*manas*); the eighth, store consciousness (*ālayavijñāna*); the ninth, pure consciousness (淨識 *amalavijñāna*).[345]

---

344 大般涅槃經疏 *Da bannieban jing shu*, 'Commentary on the *Mahāparanirvāṇa-Sūtra*' 'Commentary on the Great Decease' by Guanding 灌頂 (561–632). T1767.38.0129c08.

345 The explanation of the notion of the ninth consciousness was consummated in the *Vajrasamādhi-Sūtra* 金剛三昧經 (T 273), after which it became a fundamental doctrinal stance in such schools as Huayan 華嚴 and Tiantai 天台, and a de facto underpinning of much of Chan discourse. *Amalavijñāna* is transliterated as 阿末羅識, 菴摩羅

The interpretations are fivefold: the first is the intrinsic nature (識自相 unique characteristic) of consciousness, referring to the part of consciousness being self-aware [of perceiving the object] (識自證分);[346] The second [interpretation] is consciousness changing/distorting [the object perceived], since all objective phenomena (一切境界) arise in/from and are actualised by (現) consciousness. The third is the consciousness concomitant with [other mental factors] (識相應), since sensation and perception and other mental states of the dharma of consciousness occur at the same time. The fourth is the consciousness of derived conditions [of consciousness] (識分位). The four consciousnesses [mentioned] above are [all] equal. The fifth is the consciousness of the true form of things (thusness), explained as the thusness of the two kinds of emptiness (detachment from self and from phenomena) which is the consciousness of the true nature [of reality].

From all the above teachings, none are apart from consciousness; their collective name is 'Only Consciousness'. Therefore, be they known as characteristics, or as the [true] nature, as objective phenomena, as consciousness, as well as distinctive phases, all is 'Only Consciousness'. It is not excluded from expansion or contraction. Its aspects are general and specific at the same time, like emptiness supporting clouds and mist.

As great billowing waves of a surging ocean, again, ancient worthies describe it in detail as 'Only Consciousness'; their interpretations consist of ten aspects – elucidating the two characters, 'Only' and 'Consciousness' by initially separating the explanations, then by joining them together. First then, is the separate explanation, beginning with 'only' and after that, 'consciousness'.

To begin with the character 'only', there are three interpretations. The first is the interpretation to choose and to maintain (揀持). Choice refers to selecting and letting go of that which is grasped as self and phenomena. To maintain

識, 唵摩羅識, and 庵摩羅識; and translated as 無垢識, 清淨識, and 如來識. (for DDB sources see under 阿摩羅識). See also Radich, Michael, "Ideas about 'Consciousness' in Fifth and Sixth Century Chinese Buddhist Debates", pp. 471–512.

346 The four parts 分 of cognition according to Yogācāra Buddhism: that which is seen (objective part) 相分, that which sees 見分 (subjective part); the confirmation of that seeing 自證分 (self-aware part, self-witnessing aspect); and, the acknowledgment of that confirmation 證自證分 (reconfirming self-aware part, re-witnessing aspect).

means maintaining and holding fast by relying on the perfection / fulfilment of the two natures (持取依圓二性).[347] The *Only Consciousness Treaty* says,

> 'Only' is interpreted as isolating (遣離) consciousness from self and phenomena; it is not that there is nothing that does not separate (離) the cognising consciousness (識心) from that which is the unconditioned, and so on.'[348]

The second interpretation concerns [the two characters] 'definitive' (決) and 'meditation / calm' (定). Definitive (決 = 真理 reality principle): there are no perceptual objects independent of consciousness; meditation / calm (定=俗事): there is an inner consciousness [of / in] consciousness. The small vehicle's position posits an objective realm independent of consciousness and clearly refutes the existence of the inner consciousness (清辯破無內心).[349]

As to the third interpretation, revealing the superior, it refers to the superiority of the sovereign consciousness (心王), whilst the mental functions (心所) and the rest are subordinate. Presently only the superior is shown, not the subordinate. The *Twenty Verses on Only Consciousness* says, 'This is called "Only Consciousness" – it simply takes up the sovereign superiority [of consciousness], that "principle" is combined with the mental functions. It is like saying the sovereign is coming – it is not that there are no ministers and officials in attendance.'[350]

Next is to elucidate the word 'consciousness', which means, to understand the specific interpretation. It refers to the eight kinds of sovereign consciousnesses, namely, the intrinsic nature of consciousness and so on. The one hundred dharmas are divided into five categories.[351] Principle and phenomena are united, **[437a]** nothing being apart from consciousness. It is not that thusness

---

[347] Relative and absolute, *or*, grasper and grasped.

[348] T1585.31.0038c24; T1861.45.0260a17 (遣=遮), but following T2016.48.0436c22 (遮=遣).

[349] 二決定義. 故舊中邊頌云 此中定有空 於彼亦有此 謂俗事中定有真理. 真理中定有俗事 識表之中此二決定 顯無二取. (中定= *dhyānāntara*). T1861.45.0260a18. See also X49.0815.0714a21. The translation is tentative.

[350] T1861.45.0260a23.

[351] According to the Yogācāra 唯識 School, all experiential phenomena are divided into the five categories of: consciousness 心法, mental factors 心所, form 色法, factors not directly associated with consciousness 心不相應行法, and unconditioned dharmas 無為法. In the consciousness group there are eight consciousnesses 八識. Muller, DDB.

ought not to be 'Only Consciousness': taking in the remainder and returned to consciousness, collectively established as the name consciousness. A sutra says, 'The three realms are "Only Consciousness."'[352]

Next is to bring together explanations of 'Only Consciousness.' 'Only' refers to selection-removal: it makes the distinction that there are no external objects (遮無外境). [Yet] objects are not non-existent, as consciousness is able to perceive [them] (境無非有識能了別) – explained as the existence of an inner consciousness. Consciousness is not non-existent (心有非無): combined they are called 'Only Consciousness', 'Only' refers to the distinction that non-Being is function[ing] (唯謂遮無是用); 'Consciousness' expresses the explanation that Being is essence (識表詮有是體). United, function returns to essence: 'only' just means 'consciousness' (唯即識).

Compound terms (持業釋)[353] are among six kinds of compound words[354] [which can express] the succinct mystery of the dharma teachings. So now the characteristics of desire and the [true] nature (欲性相) can both be debated. Briefly, to cite two interpretations [aspects] of the compounds, they can be taken up in the present text.

As to the first interpretation, there are two aspects: the first is the adjective/adverb-noun compound (持業), the second is [two nouns in] apposition (同依). Concerning the first [adjective/adverb-noun compound], the adjective/adverb (持) means to maintain, preserve, support (任持); the second element (業) [of the compound] refers to the functioning, action, [regarding] karmic activity (業用). If the dharma essence can support the functioning [of karma], the functioning can reveal the essence; [so the meaning of this compound] is [literally] called 'supporting karma' (持業). It is tantamount to calling it the *ālayavijñāna* (藏識 store[house] consciousness). Consciousness is the essence, the storehouse [its] functioning. The consciousness essence can sup-

---

352 T1585.31.0039a07.

353 持業釋, (Skt. *karma-dhāraya*) [lit. 'action-carrying'] – a compound in which the first element is an adjective or adverb, and the second element a noun or adjective, respectively ('high mountain,' 'very high'). May also indicate two nouns in apposition, referring to the equality of dependence of both terms, e.g., 大乘 Mahāyāna, 'great' and 'vehicle', both equally essential to Mahāyāna with its specific meaning; also written 同依釋. See Fazang, T1585.31.009b09. DDB: Billy Brewster *et al.* Regarding Chinese Buddhist exegetes' knowledge of Sanskrit, see Teng Weijen, 'On Kuiji's Sanskrit Compound Analyses' in *Buddhism Across Asia,* pp. 173–192.

354 六合釋 (六離釋) six interpretations of compound [Sanskrit] terms.

port the functioning of the *ālayavijñāna* and just this takes the name 'supporting karma' (持業); or again, it is as if the ineffable Dharma were a lotus flower
(如妙法即蓮華), and so on.

Concerning the second interpretation, [of 持業釋, the appositional compound 同依], that is, many functions equally reliant on the one essence – tantamount to saying that a [worldling's] fragmentary life and death (分段生死)
is [in] the [coarse] body.[355] The transformation of birth and death (變易生死) is
precisely of both [in] the body.[356] Birth and death by [inconceivable] transformation (變易生死) that is, the body and so on (即身等) therefore all the myriad
dharmas take consciousness as the essence. The myriad dharmas are the functioning [of essence], the dharmas are not apart from consciousness, functioning
is not apart from essence. Consciousness – essence is able to support myriad
dharmas, for the dharmas are just this consciousness, functioning just this
essence – called the 'supporting- karma compound/interpretation'(?) (持業釋).

If no dharmas could be obtained by support from/maintaining (任持) one's
own consciousness (*sva citta* 自心), no dharmas could be established. Again, if
there were no dharmas, then there would be no functioning of karma; with no
functioning [of karma] the revealing of essence would not be possible. Therefore, know that all dharmas are consciousness; consciousness is all dharmas.
Essence and function complement each other, [they are] not one, not two.

Concerning the second compound 'to depend on and stay' (依主釋),[357]
there are two [aspects]: the first is a principal and qualifying compound; the
second is [the alternative rendering of the same] compound (依士釋), containing a principal and qualifying component. Concerning [the compound] 'depend
and stay' (依主): objective superior dharma elucidates the subordinate (inferi-
or), adopting the subordinate to show the name of the superior. It is like discussing visual consciousness: the eye is the objective basis which is relied upon, it is
the superior, whilst [eye] consciousness subjectively depends [on the eye], thus
subordinate. Therefore the superior [organ of the eye] is explained by the subordinate [eye] consciousness. Via the subordinate the superior is approached,
for the purpose of defining its name as visual consciousness: that is [an inter-

---

[355] The coarse body of fragmentary cyclic existence.

[356] A subtle, limitless body, called miraculous transformation 變易; literally, the inconceivable transformations of birth and death 不思議變易生死.

[357] 依主釋 (依士釋) (Skt. *tat-puruṣa*) – dependent compound, in which the first noun
modifies the second noun.

pretation of] the 'depend and stay compound.' Perhaps there is another, simpler understanding – 'depend and stay' [in this sense] is just another name for superior, named in common with subordinate (通名劣).

As to the second [aspect] (依士釋) [of the] 'depend and stay compound' (依主釋), it refers to the subordinate dharmas being the superior dharma's higher-level functioning (士用 'heroic performance'). Now, to explain the subordinate dharma with respect to the superior dharma: the superior dharma goes with the subordinate dharma by designating its name (彰名), as if to say that the unconditioned [is reached] as cessation [of afflictions] by analytical insight (擇滅無為).[358] Cessation by analytical insight as the conditioned is subordinate, the unconditioned being superior; it takes the superior simply by means of showing the subordinate by name. The interpretation of the [compound] 'depend and stay' is [then] the knowledge that the sovereign consciousness is the superior. All dharmas whatsoever are dharmas of consciousness. Again, consciousness is the objective support, thus superior. The dharmas are the subjective support, thus subordinate. By means of the subordinate the superior is revealed, since the dharma of consciousness is [expressed] precisely [in the compound] 'depend and stay.' So there is not a single dharma that does not belong to consciousness. If all dharmas are revealed through consciousness, [**437b**] it is due to the subordinate revealing the superior. Therefore, the dharma of consciousness [in this interpretation] is just the 'depend and stay compound.' That is why, within the inner mirror of the [Chan] teaching (宗鏡內), in supporting karma (持業) there is wealth relying on the sovereign (有財依主). Higher-level functioning (士用 'heroic performance') is immediately (隣近) carried / included within six the enumerative compound terms, which do not issue [only] from the two compounds [above] of 'upholding karma' and 'depend and stay' etc. The section below does not further explain each term in detail – taking one example will naturally avoid confusion.

437b04

Question: These statements only make the distinction (遮) that external objects do not exist; [but] there are distinctions between objects being separate from consciousness and objects not being separate from consciousness.

---

[358] 擇滅無為 destruction of afflictions through analytical meditation as unconditioned, one of six cognitive factors within the Yogacara scheme of one hundred factors which are not karmically conditioned.

Answer: Supposing that were so, why the misplaced difficulties? Both [suppositions] are at fault. If a distinction (遮) is made that objects are separate (離) from consciousness [then] there is nothing left (無餘 final). [If] there is no separation present from the objective image of cognition (相分) in consciousness, why is it called 'Only Consciousness' and not called 'only object consciousness' (唯境識)? If the distinction is made that there is no separation between consciousness and objects, this does not hold ([the distinction] is non-existent) – then transformation would only occur in a three-part [division of an instance of consciousness] (三分).[359] It is the lack of the transformative factor (變相) of the objective image of cognition (相分, that which is seen) that is at fault, so why the omission? The answer: that which is called 'Only Consciousness' makes the distinction that objects do not exist outside of consciousness, but does not make the distinction that internal objects are not separate objective aspects of consciousness as being non-existent (不遮內境不離識相分是無).

Question: [Given that] internal objects are part of consciousness, and since, moreover, it is not [that they are] non-existent, why then say that it is 'Only Consciousness,' [why] not say 'only object consciousness' (唯境識)?

Answer: It is because bodhisattvas who protect the Dharma say that the names of objects are common to both internal and external [objects], referred to as objects being separate from consciousness and objects not being separate from consciousness. Fearful of the stress laid upon external objects, the talk is simply of 'Only Consciousness', which is why the *Treatise on Only Consciousness* says,

> It means that all foolish people's attachments are to external objects, giving rise to afflictive karma and the cycle of birth and death; they do not understand the contemplative consciousness (觀心).[360]

---

[359] 四分 Four parts of cognition: that which is seen (mental phenomena), that which sees (discriminating such phenomena); the confirmation of that seeing (the power that discriminates); and, the acknowledgment of that confirmation (the verification of that power). DCBT: 171.

[360] T1585.31.0059a09.

It does not refer to the internal image of the object of cognition (相分) – tantamount to externality being totally non-existent (如外都無).

Question: The 'nature of Only Consciousness' and 'Only Consciousness' – are these the same or different?

Answer: Each has two interpretations. In the case of the two interpretations of 'the nature of Only Consciousness', the first interpretation is a counterfeit 'nature of Only Consciousness' – it is actually the nature of an all-pervasive conceptualising (subjective ideation), which [by virtue of its activity] expels purity. The second interpretation: it is the authentic 'nature of Only Consciousness,' which is really the perfectly complete true nature [of thusness], that which actualises purity.

As for what is said concerning the two interpretations of [the second case] of 'Only Consciousness', in the first [interpretation], the conventional understanding of 'Only Consciousness' is that that which stops (cuts off) purity is due to (dependent on) the arising of other [factors]. The second [interpretation of 'Only Consciousnesses'] is the superior one, namely, the consummation of reality that has obtained purity.

It is also said that characteristics and 'the nature of Only Consciousness' (唯識性相) are not the same. A characteristic is dependent on something else. Simply, it is conditioned, whether contaminated or uncontaminated (通漏無漏). The [Only Consciousness] nature is the perfectly complete – it is simply / only 'thusness'. Unconditioned, uncontaminated, it is also called, simply / only 'consciousness'. This is interpreted as discernment: the meaning is that the five stages, the one-hundred dharmas of the principles [of the teachings], coupled to phenomena, are not apart from consciousness. Now, all included in consciousness, collectively these are referred to by the name 'consciousness'. Therefore, the myriad dharmas arise from consciousness; this being so, consciousness is not only of a single human nor is it only one consciousness; still less are there other consciousnesses – and so on.

Concerning the emergence of the 'Only Consciousness' essence: first, that which is contemplated emerging from essence takes the five stages and the one hundred dharmas as the essence because contemplation is permeated by conditioned and unconditioned dharmas [alike], which implies (即) taking consciousness and characteristics as the nature of consciousness. Combined as the 'essence of Only Consciousness' none is therefore apart from consciousness.

Second, concerning the subjective contemplation emerging from essence, it is just taking consciousness and the mental functions of consciousness (心所) as the essence. The mental functions of consciousness and [437c] consciousness are therefore in a permanent association, which means, it is merely subjective, not objective.

If it is about the view/contemplation of (觀) 'Only Consciousness', then it takes wisdom from the realm of objects (於境中) as the essence; it inclines to the contemplation of the object since analytical acumen/contemplative investigation (觀察) is superior. And so it is clear that there are distinctions in 'Only Consciousness' and collectively all [these distinctions consist of] causal conditions and principle, which are of ten kinds.

The **first** [of the ten kinds of causal conditions and principle]: it rejects the false and preserves the true meaning. To reject is to do away with; false is the incorrect (虛妄). Contemplating attachments with subjective ideation (遍計) is merely falsehood arising, all without essence and function; it should be correctly removed. Due to existence of deluded feelings, principle is lacking; it means the existence [of deluded feelings] remains. The real is referred to as truly existent; that is, it contemplates the conditioned and the perfect unconditioned of dharmas (依圓法), essence as really existent; in fact, later there were two [kinds of] cognition with its objects (智境), which should be correctly maintained, because principle exists and [deluded] discrimination does not, precisely because all worldlings of the small vehicle, from beginningless time are deludedly attached to the self and to the existence of dharmas. They evidently dispute with the bodhisattvas and others, mistakenly denying the emptiness of principle and phenomena. Now, in the contemplation of 'Only Consciousness' are those who expel the false (unreal) and [engage in] contemplating emptiness; they reject the attachment to existence [of a self and dharmas] [whilst] those who maintain the real with fine analysis (有觀) [even] reject attachment to emptiness. It is neither [a question of] existence, nor of emptiness – the Dharma does not discriminate, is far from wordy explanations.

Concerning the **second** [of the ten kinds of causal conditions and principle], the meaning is the expulsion of confusion and the retention of dependently arisen subjective awareness (捨濫留純義). To give up willingly (捨) is to discard. Overflowing (濫) is confusion. To retain means to keep; pure is without admixtures. Given the contemplation of phenomena and principle, there are objects and there is consciousness. As consciousness does not arise by itself, it relies on the object and then comes to life. The object does not arise of itself but consciousness changes/adapts [to] it and then it arises (識變方起). Because of the object there is confusion; to discard it is not considered 'only' (捨之不稱唯). Since consciousness essence is pure, to retain is called 'Only Consciousness'. Therefore the *Treatise on Only Consciousness* says,

> Consciousness (我=識) only exists internally, objects also penetrate [to] the external world; fearing the confusion with external objects (境=故), it is simply spoken of as 'Only Consciousness'.[361]

It is not [only] as internal objects, as if the external is totally non-existent. The *Huayan Sutra* says, 'The three realms are only consciousness.'[362]

The **third** meaning [of the ten kinds of causal conditions and principle] is 'to gather the branches and return to the root.' 'Gathering' refers to tying together, 'branches' is seeing (i.e., the part that cognises) and the objective part of cognition (object cognised) (見相二分); 'return' is to tend toward (take refuge in); 'root' refers to the self-authenticating aspect of consciousness, because it is the foundation (所依) of essence. Now, to gather the branches and see the objective returns it to the root, the self-authenticating (validating) aspect of essence; therefore it is called 'Only Consciousness', which is why the *Sutra of the Explication of the Underlying Meaning* says,

> All perceptual objects of consciousness are manifestations of 'Only Consciousness'.[363]

The **fourth** meaning [of the ten kinds of causal conditions and principle] conceals the subordinate and reveals the superior. It refers to the sovereignty of [mental functions concomitant with consciousness ([心] 王) as] revealing the object together with the subject (王所俱能示現). The mental functions are subordinate, since they arise dependent on others. Consciousness as sovereign is superior since it conceals the inferior and does not grasp, for its basis is essence,

[361] T1585.31.0059a10.
[362] T1735.35.0789c20.
[363] T0676.16.0698b02.

so it is called 'Only Consciousness'; that is, the name reveals its superiority. The *Zhuangyan lun* says,

> Allowing that consciousness resembles two manifestations
> In this way it could resemble craving, and so on[364]

The **fifth** [of the ten kinds of causal conditions and principle] has the meaning of rejecting characteristics and realising (證) the [true] nature. Consciousness can be represented as expressing (識言所表) possession of both phenomena and principle. Phenomena refer to characteristics and functions, rejected, not grasped. Principle is the essence nature (體性), which should be sought in order to realise it. Therefore a verse in the *Summary of the Great Vehicle* says,

> On the basis of a rope arising, a snake is understood
> Insight into the rope knows that it is non-existent
> Realisation is that it is clearly seen
> Only then is it known that clarity was compromised[365]

The **sixth** interpretation [of the ten kinds of causal conditions and principle] concerns the object, meaning that it is the object that is contemplated. Consciousness is the subjective consciousness (or, is consciousness's subjective viewpoint 識即能觀心); this is the object that is contemplated. Since consciousness manifests forms, the object is not separate from consciousness. It establishes the object with reference to 'Only Consciousness'. The *Abhidharma-Sūtra* says, [**438a**] 'What ghosts, humans, deities and others see is different for each one.'[366]

The **seventh** interpretation [of the ten kinds of causal conditions and principle] concerns the teachings, that is, the capacity to expound the teachings, therefore the stated interpretation that there is 'Only Consciousness.' A verse from the *Laṅkāvatāra-Sūtra* says,

---

[364] T1585.31.0036c27 quoting T1604 莊嚴論.

[365] Not found in 攝大乘論, T1592–1594. Quotation taken from, 般若波羅蜜多心經幽贊 *Banruo boluomi duoconsciousness jing youzan*, 'Profound Explanation of the *Prajñāpāramitā* Heart Sutra' by Kuiji 窺基. T1710.33.0527b03 *etc.*

[366] Not extant. Quoted in T1585.31.0011a03.

Due to the attachment of one's own consciousness
Consciousness seems to be led around by externals (境轉)
[Yet] that which is seen does not exist
It is therefore called only consciousness (唯心)[367]

The **eighth** interpretation [of the ten kinds of causal conditions and princi-
ple] concerns principle] (道理). Principle is 'Only Consciousness'; a verse in the
Discourse on the Theory of Only Consciousness says,

These are all transformations of consciousness
Discriminating that which discriminates
Because of 'this and that' being non-existent
Everything is therefore 'Only Consciousness' (唯識)[368]

The **ninth** interpretation [of the ten kinds of causal conditions and principle]
concerns practice. Practice refers to the practice of contemplative [insight / ana-
lytical] meditation (觀行), that is, when a bodhisattva has established the stage
of working on the four meditations and so forth,[369] namely, the practice of [ana-
lytical] contemplation and concentration. All [these practices] are not separate
from consciousness. A verse in the *Yogâcārabhūmi-śāstra* says, 'A bodhisattva
is established in the stage of contemplating the object as only being consciousness'[370]

The **tenth** interpretation [of the ten kinds of causal conditions and prin-
ciple] concerns the result (fruit, Skt. *phala*), referred to as the four cognitions
of Buddhahood.[371] Bodhisattvas possess merit-producing powers, none sepa-

---

[367] Quoted in T1585.31.0010c09.

[368] T1585.31.0038c16.

[369] 四尋伺觀等 the four contemplations of initial application and susequent investigation
(?). 四觀 = 四念住, the four bases of mindfulness. DDB: in the *Yogâcārabhūmi-śāstra*
there is another set of four bases: observation of consciousness's appropriation 觀心執
受; observation of consciousness's reception 觀心領納; observation of consciousness's
discrimination [of objects] 觀心了別, and observation of consciousness's pollution and
purity 觀心染淨. T 1579.30.582c23.

[370] Not found in T1579; 菩薩於定位 觀影唯是心 in T1585.31.0049b29.

[371] The great perfect mirror cognition; cognition of the nature of equality of all dharmas;
ineffable observing cognition; cognition with unrestrained activity.

146

rate from consciousness. Therefore the *Zhuangyan lun* says, 'Thusness is consciousness without an object, it is the realm of purity without outflows' etc. [372]

These are the above ten interpretations on the cognition of the [true] nature, characteristics, objects, cognition and on the teachings, the principle, practises and [their] results, all are nothing but consciousness. There is not a single dharma that is not mentioned, therefore it is styled as the sovereign of enlightened interpretation of all sutras, relied on by all the sages as the father. If someone were to encounter it, then seeking would suddenly be at an end, for there is not a single dharma that can be sought (or, not a single dharma but can be sought 無一法而可求); there is not a single thing lacking – all attain the Tathāgata's unexcelled treasure. Would it be rather the same as the unpolished gem in a thorny mountain cave (荊岫璞)? Could the teachings of the oceanic hidden spiritual gem, already investigated, be compared to that under the jaws of the awesome black dragon? It is followed up by the complete exhaustion of sentient beings' sufferings, the severance of the root sickness of the afflictions. One thought-moment accomplishes the self-correction of all the thousand byways, and so the *Lotus Sutra* says,

> It is like a clear cool pool able to satisfy all those thirsts and deficiencies; like one who is cold coming to the fire; like one naked acquiring clothing; like a merchant becoming a lord; like a son acquiring a mother; like crossing water by acquiring a boat; like sickness finding a cure; like darkness obtaining light; like coming into riches from poverty; like the people obtaining a sovereign; like a businessman gaining an ocean; like a torch banishing darkness. This *Lotus Sutra* is also like this; it can facilitate sentient beings' freedom from all suffering, from all illnesses and pains, is able to set free the bonds of birth and death.[373]

Therefore it should be known that only this is truly real. The ten thousand things are all empty. This is the acme of the teachings, of rank unequalled. As the *Guangfa jing* says,

> There was a bodhisattva by the name of Shangshou (the Highest Rank) who became an alms-beggar [monk]. He entered a city begging for alms. At that

---

[372] Quoted in T1735.35.0878a17.

[373] T0262.09.0054b14.

time there was a monk by the name of Hengqie (Persistently Attending), who addressed the alms-beggar, saying, 'Where have you come from?'

'I have come from the truly real,' answered the alms-beggar.

'What is meant by the truly real?'

'Because it is quiescent (寂滅) it is called "truly real",' answered the alms-beggar.

'Among the characteristics of the truly real, what is to be sought, what is not to be sought?' asked the monk.

'Nothing is to be sought.'

'As to there being nothing to seek, what use would it be to seek?' asked the monk.

'Within there being nothing to seek I nevertheless seek it,' replied the alms-beggar.

'In the absence of anything to seek, what need would there be to seek?'

'As to there being something to seek, all is emptiness; [**438b**] attaining is also empty; attachments are also empty; the real is also empty; coming is also empty; words are also empty; questions are also empty; the tranquillity of nirvana – all boundless emptiness and yet again all empty. I thus follow the order / sequence of [? for attaining] the dharma of emptiness (次第空法), then search the truly real (而求真實),' said the alms-beggar.[374]

Therefore it should be known that if it is possible to search emptiness in every dharma, then within every entrance is liberation. When man and dharmas, questions and answers and verbal expressions come and go [then] it is like images in the mirror of the teachings (宗鏡中像). If *prajñā*-wisdom illuminates the calm extinction (寂滅) of nirvana, that is likened to the clarity in the mirror of the teachings. Therefore, whether image or clarity, all is completely empty. There is only mirror and essence (or the body / essence of the mirror 鏡體), a perpetual disclosure (恒常披露) everywhere and has never been [inconstantly] appearing and disappearing. Therefore it is said that 'I thus follow the order / sequence of [for attaining] the dharma of emptiness then search the truly real,' – that is, to know all dharmas, since all are truly real. 'In the absence of

---

374 止觀輔行傳弘決 *Zhiguan fuconsciousnessg zhuan hongjue*, by Zhanran 湛然 (711–782). A commentary on T1911 摩訶止觀 'The Great Śamatha-Vipaśyanā [practices]' by Zhiyi 智顗. T1912.46.0191a05.

there being anything to seek, I seek it anyway.'[375] Furthermore, a person who seeks the Dharma in all dharmas should not be seeking for anything (無所求). Great master Rong also said, 'If there were a single dharma that could be obtained, that would be the time of searching for right and wrong.'[376] Therefore the *Vimalakirti Sūtra* says,

> [Again Mañjuśri] asks, 'Where should emptiness be sought?' [Vimalakirti] answers: 'It should be sought in the sixty-two kinds of [wrong] views.'[377] Again [Mañjuśri], 'Where should the sixty-two kinds of [wrong] views be sought?' 'They should be sought in the liberation of all the Tathāgatas,' replied Vimalakirti. [Mañjuśri] again, 'Where should the liberation of the all Tathāgatas be sought?' 'It should be sought in the activity of consciousness of all sentient beings,' answered Vimalakirti.'[378]

An old commentary says,

> 'The wisdom/cognition of emptiness is due to insight/views arising; the wisdom of emptiness then, lacks a self-nature (無性) and without a self-nature, wisdom is therefore empty.'[379]

Just this is called the wisdom of emptiness. Wrong views based on (因) the liberation of all the Tathāgatas still exist; wrong causes come to correction and wrong views too are empty. The liberation of all the Tathāgatas causes the awakening of sentient beings. The activity of [their] consciousness then, is the emptiness of liberation, that is, it accords with this emptiness and essence which are not two. Therefore, conjointly seeking principle (互求理), there is no place it does not pervade.

The explanation: wrong and right, since the essence is originally the same, the principle of emptiness too has never been hidden for a moment. If, in this

---

[375] T1735.35.0647c11.

[376] Chan master Farong (594–697 CE), 1st patriarch of the Oxhead [Niutou] school of Chan.

[377] See *Sutra on the Brahmā's Net of Sixty-two Views (Brahmajāla Sutta)* 梵網六十二見經.T21.01.

[378] 維摩結經 '*Vimalakīrti-nirdeśa-Sūtra*' translated by Kumarajiva 鳩摩羅什 (344–414 CE). T0475.14.0544c04.

[379] T1736.36.0528c11.

equality of the [true] nature there is just no urge to seek, it is solely for the sake of those who do not yet know that we talk of seeking. As a sutra says about non-arising,

> The vow to seek after the wisdom of all the Tathāgatas is also not to be attached to the vow.[380]

Neither does seeking the wisdom of the Tathāgatas cause attachment to desire, to say nothing of its other good actions. Furthermore, because the bodhisattva is detached from the vow to seek, it is simply that sentient beings do not know how to seek the Buddha Way that the bodhisattva therefore arouses the vow, saying simply, 'I vow to seek the Buddha's Way.' Sentient beings, because of this, know then to give rise in consciousness to seek the Buddha's Way, attaining for themselves the aim to know that there is nothing to seek.

As explained above then, every thought moment is associated with the true original nature (實相), with no further residual thoughts. Therefore the *Laṅkâvatāra-Sūtra* says, 'Each of the characteristics is associated/connected (相應) and free from all wrong views.'[381] So this knowledge, concerning all characteristics is always associated with the true original nature and is naturally free from all faults. This is understood as the primary interpretation – the purified true consciousness is clearly and lucidly [438c] penetrated, yet without any attachment to thoughts; that is, neither to things nor to thusness. Only consciousness proceeds straight ahead, which is what Buddhism acknowledges – just this is the object of self-realisation. A verse in a treatise goes on to say,

> Self-knowledge precludes following others
> Silent cessation is without conceptual elaborations
> Without separation, devoid of ideation
> This then is called the true original nature (實相)[382]

---

380 思益梵天所問經 *Siyi fantian suowen jing,* 'Sutra of the Questions of Viśeṣa-cinti-brahma' translation by Kumārajīva 鳩摩羅什 (CE 402). T0586.15.0053a02.

381 T0671.16.0521a29 / T0672.16.0592c25.

382 中論 (中觀論) *Madhyamaka-śāstra* attributed to Nāgârjuna translated by Kumārajīva in 409CE. T1564.30.0024a07.

Question: Approximately how many kinds of these 'Only Consciousnesses' are there?

Answer: In short, there are two kinds: the first encompasses the whole (具分), the second does not encompass the whole. In the case of 'Only Consciousness' encompassing the whole, it is due to the principle: no intrinsic self-nature (以無性理故), which becomes the interpretation of thusness obeying conditions – such that non-arising and non-cessation is combined with (in harmony with 和合) arising and cessation, [but] it is neither the same nor different. It is called the *ālayavijñāna*, meaning, it encompasses the whole.

If there is not a complete reliance on the true consciousness, if phenomena do not rely on principle, then the only concern is with arising and cessation and in that case is not the encompassing whole. It is said,

There is an [essence] quality shadowed outside (影外有質)[383], as being in-complete (半頭half of) 'Only Consciousness'; [raw sensate] quality (質) and shadow-image are both shadow-image, serving as encompassing the whole. This is the encompassing whole within the 'Only Consciousness' teaching (宗).[384]

Furthermore, if there is the certitude of deep faith in the correct principles of this 'Only Consciousness', then there will be a speedy arrival at bodhi (awakening). It is like mounting a chariot and installed (*or* quickly) reaching a distant place; like boarding a boat and seated, advancing to the other shore. As the *Jewel-Arising Treatise* says, 'It refers to reliance on the great vehicle [of the Mahāyāna] establishing three realms; put simply, it/there is only consciousness (但唯是識).'[385]

The explanation: it is as the sutras aver, speaking of the great vehicle it refers to the path practised by the bodhisattva, reaching the excellent spiritual attainment as a result of this. Cultivating the contemplation [of the principle of]

[383] *Zhi yin* 質影 raw sensate appearance and the shadow/image/reflection thus derived.

[384] T1736.36.0073b29.

[385] 成唯識寶生論 *Cheng weishi baoshenglun*, 'Jewel-Arising Treatise on Setting Forth Consciousness-Only' Dharmapāla's interpretation of Vasubandhu's Twenty Verses on Consciousness-Only, translation by Yijing 義淨 (635–713). T1591.31.0077b22.

'Only Consciousness' (修唯識觀), it is the faultless correct path of expedient means because this kind of path shows up those expedient means. In all the sutras there are various kinds of defining activities (行相), extensively explaining the teachings: such as earth, water, fore and air, combined they sustain [all] things (并所持物) [though some] classifications are difficult to understand fully. Directions and places then become limitless and because of this clear discernment (審知) the characteristics of one's own consciousness become manifest. Then, progressing to many places and abandoning their external marks, far removed from joy and sorrow, once again there is the perception of the existence of the ocean: clamour and stillness are not different. [The bodhisattva] abandons other lesser ways, for they sever the hope for the great vehicle and are attended by all kinds of addictions, perceived as a dangerous precipice. Becoming deeply fearful, correctly he is destined for the middle way.

If it is acknowledged that it is one's own consciousness that fabricates [projections, then] there are no limits to the endowments (資糧), which are easy to accumulate without waiting a long time. It is like using minimal effort in the ability to achieve great things. Good wayfaring, in all places, [is] as if in the palm of one's hand. Because of this principle, that which is wished for can be fulfilled according to intention and then can transform.

End of Fascicle Four

Appendix One

Yongming Yanshou's sources
Fascicles Two / Three / Four
Records from the Ancestral Mirror

B14n0081 雙峰山曹侯溪寶林傳 *Shuang feng shan cao houxi Baolinzhuan*, 'Biographies from Baolin Temple, Mnt. Shuangfeng, Caohouxi'. A ten-fascicle (incomplete) collection of biographies of Chan masters at Baolinsi 寶林寺 by Zhiju 智炬 in 801CE.

F28.1983 漩澓偈 *Xuanfu ji*, by Dharma master Dushun (557–640) 杜順法師, first patriarch of the *Huayan* lineage.

T210–213.4 法句經 *Faju jing*, (Skt. Dharmapada, Pāli. Dhammapada); 'Dharma-phrase Sutra' transliterated as 曇鉢經. 2 fasc. by Dharmatrāta 法救, T 210.4.559–574. Translated by Vighna 維祇難 et al. A collection of phrases comprising the basic teachings of Buddhist morality. The Chinese version contains 758 verses. Sometimes known as the Pseudo-Dharmapāda. There are four Chinese translations, dated CE 224, 290–306, 399, 980–1001.

T0220.05–7   大般若波羅蜜多經   *Da   Bore   Boluo   Miduo   Jing*, *Mahāprajñāpāramitā-Sūtra*, translated by Xuanzang 玄奘 from 660–663. This massive work, filling three entire Taishō volumes, is the largest of any Buddhist text, comprising nearly 50,000,000 characters in the Chinese translation contained in the Taishō canon.

T0231.08   勝天王般若經 *Shengtianwang   bore   jing, Pravara-deva-rāja-pariprcchā* (勝天王般若波羅蜜經). Translation by Upaśūnya / Ūrdhvaśūnya, 月婆首那 Indian, son of a king (565 CE), a *Prajñāpāramitā* text taught in Rājagrha to King Pravara-deva.

T0262.09   妙法蓮華經   *Miaofa lianhua jing, Saddharmapuṇḍarīka-Sūtra*, 'Sutra of the Lotus of the Wonderful Dharma', translated by Kumārajīva in 406 CE.

T0273.09 金剛三昧經 *Jingang sanmei jing*, *Vajrasamādhi-Sūtra* (possibly composed in Korea).

T278.10 大方廣佛華嚴經 *Dafangguangfo huayan jing*, *Buddhâvataṃsaka-mahāvaipulya-Sūtra*. The first full translation by Buddhabhadra 佛陀跋陀羅 c.420 in sixty fascicles.

T0279.10 大方廣佛華嚴經 *Dafangguangfo huayan jing*, *Buddhâvataṃsaka-mahāvaipulya-Sūtra* translated by Śikṣānanda 實叉難陀 c.699 in eighty fascicles.

T0310.11 大寶積經 *Da baoji jing*, *Mahāratnakūṭa-Sūtra* translated by Bodhiruci *et al*, a collection of Mahāyāna sutras based on sermons given by the Buddha at forty-nine assemblies.

T0340.12 文殊師利所說不思議佛境界經 *Wenshushili suoshuo busiyi fojingjie jing*, 'Sutra of Mañjuśrī's Explanation of the Inconceivable Buddha-realm'. Translation by Bodhiruci 菩提流志 (572?–727) in 693 CE.

T0342.12 如幻三昧經 *Ruhuan sanmei jing*, 'The As-if-Samadhi were Illusion Sūtra'. Translation by Dharmarakṣa 竺法護 (239–316).

T353.12 勝鬘經 *Shemgman Jing*, (勝鬘師子吼一乘大方便方廣經), *Śrīmālādevī-siṃha-nāda-Sūtra* translated into Chinese in 436 CE by Guṇabhadra 求那跋陀羅 (394–468).

T0374.12 大般涅槃經 *Da banniepan jing*, *Mahāparinirvāṇa-Sūtra*, 'Sutra of the Great Decease', translated by Dharmakṣema 曇無讖 (385–433).

T0375.12 大般涅槃經 *Da banniepan jing*, *Mahāparinirvāṇa-Sūtra*, 'Sutra of the Great Decease', translated by Huiyan 慧嚴 (363–443).

T0397.13 大集經 *Daji jing*, *Mahāsaṃnipāta-Sūtra*, 'Great Collection Sutra' translated by Dharmakṣema 曇無懺 (385–433 CE) and others.

T0403.13 [no. 39 (12)] 阿差末菩薩經 *Achamo pusajing*, *Akṣayamati Pusa Jing*, 'The Sutra of Bodhisattva Akṣayamati' translated by Tripitaka master

Dharmarakṣa 三藏竺法護 (239–316 CE) of 西晉 Western Jin, 'the greatest Buddhist translator before Kumārajîva,' E. Zürcher, BCC: 65–70.

To462.14 寶篋經 *Baoqie jing*, (大乘遍照光明藏無字法門經 *Dasheng bianzhao guangmingzang wuzi famen jing*), 'Great Vehicle Sutra of the No-Letter Casket from the Store of Vairocana' (T828.17). This is actually from 大方廣寶篋經 'The Great and Broad (*vaipulya*) Jewel Box Sutra'.

To475.14 維摩結經, *Vimalakīrti-nirdeśa-Sūtra*, translated by Kumarajiva 鳩摩羅什 (344–414 CE).

To482.14 持世經 *Chishi jing*, 'Sutra of the World Upholder' translated by Kumārajīva 鳩摩羅什 (early 5th cent) – a dialogue between the Buddha and the bodhisattva World-Upholder.

To580.14 佛說長者女菴提遮師子吼了義經 *Fo shuo chang zhe nu An Tizhe shi zi houle yi jing*, 'Sutra spoken by the Buddha on the Clear Meaning of the Lion's Roar to An Tizhe daughter of an elder,' (Also known as the *Sutra of the Elder's Daughter* 長者子女經 or 長老子女經), translator unknown, 6th cent.

To586.15 思益梵天所問經 *Siyi fantian suowen jing*, 'Sutra of the Questions of Viśeṣa-cinti-brahma' Translation by Kumārajīva 鳩摩羅什 (CE 402).

T609.15 禪要經 *Chanyao jing*. 'Sutra on the Essentials of Meditation', 1 fasc., K 1012, T 609. Translator unknown: listed in the Hou Han lu 後漢錄 (25–220). Translated during the Eastern Han. Also known as the *Chanyao jing heyu pin* 禪要經訶欲品 and *Chanyao heyu jing* 禪要訶欲經. Part of the text overlaps with T 616 禪法要解, which was translated by Kumārajīva 鳩摩羅什.

To639.15 月燈三昧經 *Yuedeng sanmei jing*, 'The Discourse to Prince Candraprabha', a text on meditation, translated by Narêndrayaśas 那連提耶舍 (517–589 CE) in 557.

To650.15 諸法無行經 *Zhufawuxing jing, Sarvadharmâpravṛtti Nirdeśa Sūtra*, 'Sutra on the Karmic Non-Accumulation of all Dharmas,' translated by Kumārajīva (344–413).

T0670.16 楞伽阿跋多羅寶經 *Lengqie abaduoluo Baojing*, 'The Precious *Sūtra of Laṅkâvatāra*' Guṇabhadra's 求那跋陀羅 (394–468) partial translation.

T0671.16 入楞伽經 *Renlengjia jing, Laṅkāvatāra-Sūtra*, 'Sutra on (the Buddha's) Entering (the Country of) Lanka,' translated by Bodhiruci 菩提流支 (? –527 CE) in 513.

T0672.16 大乘入楞伽經 *Dasheng rulengqie jing*, translated by Śikṣānanda 實叉難陀 in 700.

T0676.16 解深密經 *Jie shenmi jing*, 'Sutra on Understanding Profound and Esoteric Doctrine' translated by Xuanzang; the most important scriptural source for the doctrines of the Yogacara school 瑜伽行派. T675, 677, 678, 679 by other translators.

T0681.16 大乘密嚴經 *Dacheng miyan jing, Ghanavyūha Sūtra*, 'Great Vehicle Sutra of [the Pure Land], Densely Adorned,' translated by Divākara 地婆訶羅 (613–687).

T0721.17 正法念處經 *Zhengfa nianchu jing, Saddharma-smṛty-upasthāna-Sūtra*, 'The Basis of Mindfulness of the True Dharma *Sūtra*,' translation by Gautama Prajñāruci 瞿曇般若流支 (mid. 6th cent CE).

T0815.17 佛昇忉利天爲母説法經, *Fo sheng daoli tianwei mu shuo fa jing*, 'The Sutra in which Buddha Ascends to the Heaven of the Thirty-three [celestials] to Preach the Dharma for his Mother.' trans. Dharmarakṣa.

T0839.17 占察善惡業報經 *Zhancha shan'e yebao jing*, 'Sutra on the Divination of the Effect of Good and Evil Actions.' Composed in East Asia?

T0945.19 大佛頂如來密因修證了義諸菩薩萬行首楞嚴經 *Da foding rulai miyin xiuzheng liaoyi zhupusa wanxing shoulengyan jing, Śūraṃgama-sūtra*, translated by Pramiti 般刺蜜帝 705 CE.

T1345.21 金剛場陀羅尼經 *Jingangchang tuoluoni jing*, 'Dhāraṇī of the Adamantine Place', translation by Jñānagupta 闍那崛多 (523–600 / 605?).

T1509.25 大智度論 Da Zhidu Lun, *Mahāprajñāpāramitā-śāstra*, 'Commentary on the *Mahāprajñāpāramitā-Sūtra*' attributed to Nāgârjuna, translated by Kumārajīva.

T1515.25 金剛般若波羅蜜經破取著不壞假名論, *Jingang bore boluomi jing po quzhe bu huai Jiaming lun*, *Vajracchedikā prajñāpāramitā-Sūtra śastra* on the refutation of grasping onto the indestructible, nominally established. Composed by 功德施菩薩 Guñada (?), translated by Divākara *et al* 683 CE.

T1564.30 中觀論 *Mūlamadhyamaka-kārikā*, translated by Kumārajīva 鳩摩羅什 in 409, with his own comments.

T1579.30 瑜伽師地論 *Yuqie shidi lun*, *Yogâcārabhūmi-śāstra*, 'Discourse on the Stages of Concentration Practice' translated by Xuanzang 玄奘 between 646–648 CE.

T1580.30 瑜伽師地論釋 *Yuqieshidilun shi*, *Yogâcārabhūmi-śāstra-kārikā*, 'Explanation of the Stages of Yoga Practice Treatise' by Jinaputra 最勝子, translation by Xuanzang 玄奘 in 650.

T1585.31 成唯識論 *Cheng weishi lun*, 'Discourse on the Theory of Only [Constructs of] Consciousness'. Mainly a translation by Xuanzang 玄奘 of Dharmapāla's 護法 commentary on the Thirty Verses on Consciousness-only 唯識三十頌, by Vasubandhu 世親, but it also includes edited translations of other masters' works on the same verses. It is the primary text of the Faxiang 法相 school.

T1588.31 唯識論 *Wéishì lun*, Prajñāruci's 般若流支 translation (6th century) of Vasubandhu's *Viṃśatikā-vijñapti-mātratā-siddhi* (*Viṃśatikākārikā*).

T1590.31 唯識二十論 *Weishi ershi lun*, 'Twenty Verses on Consciousness-only' by Vasubandhu 世親, translated in 661 by Xuanzang 玄奘.

T1591.31 成唯識寶生論 *Cheng weishi baoshenglun*, 'Jewel-Arising Treatise on Setting Forth Consciousness-only', Dharmapāla's interpretation of Vasubandhu's Twenty Verses on Consciousness-only, translation by Yijing 義淨 (635–713).

T1600.31, 辯中邊論 *Bian zhongbian lun, Madhyānta-vibhāga,* 'Analysis of the Middle and the Extremes' translated by Xuanzang 玄奘 (in 661).

T1604.31 大乘莊嚴經論 *Dasheng zhuangyanjing lun (Mahāyāna-sūtrâlaṃkāra)*, 'Treatise on the Scripture of Adorning the Great Vehicle', attributed to Asaṅga 無著 (4th cent.). Translated by Prabhākaramitra 波羅頗蜜多羅 CE 630－33.

T1624.31 觀所緣緣論 *Guan suoyuanyuan lun*, 'Treatise on Contemplating Objective Conditions' by Dignāga 陳那, translated by Xuanzang in 657.

T1666.32 大乘起信論 *Dasheng Qixin Lun,* The more popular translation of Aśvaghoṣa's 馬鳴 'The Awakening of Faith in the Mahāyāna' is attributed to Paramārtha 眞諦 (499–569), while the later translation (T1667) is attributed to Śikṣānanda 實叉難陀 (arrived in China 694 CE).

T1667.32 大乘起信論 *Dasheng Qixin Lun,* 'The Awakening of Faith in the Mahāyāna' by Aśvaghoṣa 馬鳴, translation is attributed to Śikṣānanda 實叉難陀 (early 8th century).

T1668.32 釋摩訶衍論 *Shi Moheyan Lun,* 'Explanation of the Treatise on Mahāyāna' (7th–8th cent.?) is a commentary on the *Awakening of Faith.* Korean?

T1710.33 般若波羅蜜多心經幽贊 *Banruo boluomi duoxin jing youzan,* 'Profound Explanation of the *Prajñāpāramitā* Heart *Sūtra*' by Kuiji 窺基.

T1716.33 妙法蓮華經玄義 *Miaofa lianhua jing xuanyi,* 'The Profound Meaning of the Sutra on the Lotus of the Marvellous Dharma'. Zhiyi's commentary on the Lotus Sutra is traditionally considered to be the most important in the Tiantai tradition.

T1730.34 金剛三昧經論 *Commentary on the Geumgang sammae gyeong,* (*Vajrasamādhi-Sūtra* T0273) by the Korean scholar-monk Wonhyo 元曉 (617–686).

T1733.35 華嚴經探玄記 *Huayanjing tanxuan ji,* 'Record of the Search for the Profundities of the Huayan Sutra' by Fazang 法藏 (643–712).

T1735.35 大方廣佛華嚴經疏 *Dafangguang fo huayan jing shu,* 'Commentary on the Flower Ornament *Sūtra*' in 60 fasc., by Chengguan 清涼澄觀 (738–839).

T1736.36 大方廣佛華嚴經隨疏演義鈔 *Dafangguang fo huayan jing suishu yanyi chao,* 'Subcommentary and explanation of the meaning of the *Buddhâvataṃsaka-mahāvaipulya-Sūtra*', Composed by Chengguan.

T1767.38 大般涅槃經疏 *Da bannieban jing shu,* 'Commentary on the *Mahāparanirvāṇa-Sūtra*', (Commentary on the Great Decease) by Guanding 灌頂 (561–632).

T1763.37 大般涅槃經集解 *Da banniepan jing jijie,* 'Collected Commentaries on the Maha-Nirvana Sutra' by Baoliang 寶亮 et al. (Liang dynasty c 509 CE).

T1777.38 維摩經玄疏 *Weimojing xuanshou,* 'Profound Commentary on the Vimalakirti Sutra' by Zhiyi 智顗 (538–597).

T1791.39 注大乘入楞伽經 A commentary by Bao Chen 寶臣 (Song dyn. n.d.) of the *Laṅkâvatāra-Sūtra* (trans. Śikṣānanda 實叉難陀 in 700, T 672.16).

T1795.39 大方廣圓覺修多羅了義經略疏註 *Dafangguang yuanjue xiuduoluo liaoyi jing lueshuzhu,* 'An Abridged Commentary to the Sutra of Perfect Enlightenment' by Zongmi 宗密 (780–841).

T1799.39 首楞嚴義疏注經 *Shoulengyan yishu zhu jing,* 'An annotated commentary on the meaning of the *Śūraṃgama-sūtra*' (n. d.) (the *Śūraṃgama-sūtra* was translated by Pramiti 般剌蜜帝705CE).

T1830.43 成唯識論述記 *Cheng weishi lun shuji,* 'A commentary on the *Cheng weishi lun*' 成唯識論 'Discourse on the Theory of Only Consciousness,' by Kuiji 窺基 (632–682 CE).

T1831.43 唯識樞要 *weishi shu yao,* 'Essentials of the Discourse on the Theory of Only Consciousness [in the Palm of the Hand]' (成唯識論掌中樞要) by Kuiji.

T1843.44 大乘起信論義疏 *Dacheng qixin lun yishu,* 'Commentary on the Awakening of Faith', attributed to (?) Huiyuan 慧遠 (523–592) of Jingying.

T1844.44 起信論疏 *Qǐ xìn lùn shū*, 'Commentary on the Awakening of Faith' by the Korean monk Wonhyo 元曉 (617–686).

T1859.45 肇論疏 *Zhaolun shu*, 'Commentary on the Zhao lun' by Yuankang 元康 (7th cent).

T1861. 45 大乘法苑義林章 *Dasheng fayuan yilin zhang*, 'Essay on the Forest of Meanings in the Dharma Grove of the Great Vehicle' by Kuiji 窺基 (632–682).

T1875.45 華嚴經義海百門 *Huayanjing yihai bomen*, 'The Hundred Gates to the Ocean of Meanings (samadhis) of the Avatamsaka Sutra' by Fazang 法藏 (643–712).

T1876.45 修華嚴奧旨妄盡還源觀 *Xiu huayan aozhi wangjinhuanyuan guan*, 'The Contemplation of the Profound Pointers of the *Huayan* Practice of Definitively Returning Delusion to the Source' by Fazang 法藏 (643–712).

T1884.45 註華嚴法界觀門 *Zhu Huayan fajie guanmen*, 'Elucidations on the Contemplation of the Huayan Dharma Realm' by Zongmi 宗密 (Guifeng 圭峰 780–841).

T1896.45 釋門歸敬儀 *Shimen guijingyi*, 'Returning to the School of Śākyamuni with Reverent Observances' by Daoxuan 道宣 (596–667).

T1911.46 摩訶止觀 *Mohe Zhiguan*, 'The great Śamatha-Vipaśyanā [practises]' by Zhiyi 智顗 (538–597 CE).

T1912.46 止觀輔行傳弘決 *Zhiguan fuxing zhuan hongjue*, by Zhanran 湛然 (711–782). A commentary on T1911.

T2009.48 小室六門 *Xiaoshi liumen*, 'Xiaoshi's Six Gates', a collection of six treatises attributed to Bodhidharma, earliest extant edition is dated 1647 from Tokugawa Japan. The individual treatises of which it is composed, however, were written in China during the Tang 唐代 (618–907).

T2058.50 付法藏因緣傳 *Fu fazang Yinyuan Zhuan*, 'Chronicle of the Successive

Transmission of the Dharma Canon,' compilers Tan Yao 曇曜, and Kivkara 吉迦夜, 5ᵗʰ cent.

X63n1231 心賦注/注心賦 *Xin fu zhu/zhu Xin fu,* 'Annotations on heart's endowment' or 'Notes on the heart in the *fu* verse form,' attributed to Master Yongming Yanshou himself.

X69n1335 善慧大士語錄 *Shanhui Dashi Yulu,* 'Recorded Sayings of the Eminent Layman Shanhui Fu Dashi'. Compiled during the Tang dynasty 唐代 (618–907) by Lou Ying 樓穎 (n. d.)

Appendix Two

From the *Jingde Chuandeng Lu*
The Tenth Generation Heirs of Chan Master Qingyuan Xingsi
Dharma Heirs of Dharma Preceptor to the Nation [of Wuyue] Tiantai Deshao

RTL: 26.921 Chan Master Hangzhou Huiri Yongming *Si* Zhijue Yanshou
Chan master Zhijue Yanshou (904–975 CE) of Huiri Yongming Temple, Hangzhou (Zhejiang) was a native of Yuhang (Zhejiang, Yuhang *shi,* Yuhang *zhen*)
whose family name was Wang. Whilst still wearing his hair in little tufts, he
dedicated his heart to the Buddha's vehicle. Since the capping ceremony (age
twenty), he partook neither of root vegetables nor of meat, eating only one meal
a day. Taking up the *Lotus Sūtra,* reading seven lines at a time, he could recite it
all within sixty days; even flocks of sheep were moved and kneeled to listen. At
the age of twenty-eight Yanshou was serving under the Military Commander
of Huating (Shanghai, Songjiang), attached to the Longce Temple, where Great
master Cuiyan Yongming (**18.490**) was incumbent, offering deep elucidations
of the profoundly transformative Dharma.

At that time Ruler Wenmu (r. 932–941 CE) of the state of Wuyue, knowing
of the master and admiring his Dao, complied with the master's aspiration by
releasing him [from military duties] in order to leave the home life and formally
take Master Cuiyan as his master. Carrying out duties for others selflessly, he
forgot himself entirely. His robes were not of silk, the food not heavily spiced;
fresh vegetables and wearing a cotton robe, so the days and nights passed.

Later, the master journeyed to the top of Mount Tianzhu, in the Tiantai
range and practised meditation there for ninety days. Quails and other little
birds came to nest in the folds of his robe. Then the master went to pay respects
to National Preceptor [De]Shao, who immediately recognised in him a deep
vessel of the Dharma and privately gave him profound pointers, saying, 'You
and the Marshal (Ruler) have an affinity link, for he daily takes delight in
Buddhist affairs.' Then the master received the seal of transmission privately.
Residing initially on Mount Xuedou in Mingzhou (Zhejiang, Ningbo), students
came to be together.

(Textual comment: In the first year of the Xianping reign era (998 CE), the temple name tablet was conferred by Imperial decree, as 'The Wealth in Sageliness Temple' (Zisheng *Si*)).

In the first year of the Jianlong reign period (960 CE) Ruler Zhongyi invited the master to occupy the newly constructed Lingyin Temple as the founding incumbent. The following year he was again invited to occupy the great Yongming Temple as the second generation incumbent [following Master Cuiyan]. The monks numbered in excess of two thousand.

The master dwelt for fifteen years in Yongming Temple, guiding some one thousand seven hundred disciples to the shore of liberation. In the 7th year of the Kaibao reign period (974 CE) he returned to Mount Tiantai to lead an ordination ceremony for more than ten thousand persons and a Bodhisattva ordination for all seven groups of Buddhists. At night food was offered to the hungry ghosts, mornings, an incalculable number of all kinds of animals were set free. Six times regularly, day and night, flowers were strewn on the paths [around the temple].

The master recited the *Lotus Sūtra* with great verve some thirteen thousand times, composed the *Zongjing Lu,* wrote verses, chants and eulogies which amounted to a hundred thousand characters, all spreading beyond the seas. When the ruler of Silla (Korea) read the master's teachings, he dispatched an emissary with a letter, declaring himself a disciple and conferred upon the master a robe weaved from gold thread, crystal beads and pearls, a golden washing bowl and other such things. Thirty-six monks from Silla personally inherited the dharma-seal and all returned to their country to propagate the Dharma, each in their own region.

In the 12th month of the 8th year of Kaibao (975 CE), corresponding to the twelfth year of the sexagenarian cycle, the master showed signs of illness and on the morning of the 26th day, after lighting incense and addressing the assembly, the master sat down cross-legged and passed away.

On the 6th day of the 1st month of the following year, the pagoda was erected on Mount Daci. The master was seventy-two years old and had been a monk for forty-two years. Emperor Taizong, by imperial decree, conferred upon the temple the name 'Chan Temple of Everlasting Tranquillity'.

Bibliography

List of Abbreviations

BCC   *The Buddhist Conquest of China,* by E. Zürcher, Leiden, 1974

CDL   *Jingde Chuandeng Lu,* 1011

DCBT   *Dictionary of Chinese Buddhist Terms,* by W.E. Soothill & L. Hodous, London, 1937

DDB   *Digital Dictionary of Buddhism,* http://www.buddhism-dict.net/ddb Charles Mueller

MMW   *Sanskrit-English Dictionary,* by M. Monier-Williams, Oxford, 1899

MT   *The Mystique of Transmission,* by Wendy L. Adamek, New York, 2007

RTL   *Records of the Transmission of the Lamp,* by Randolph S. Whitfield, (trans.), Norderstedt, 2015–2020

YYCC   *Yongming Yanshou's Conception of Chan in the Zongjing Lu, A Special Transmission within the Scriptures* by Albert Welter, Oxford, 2011

Boucher, Daniel. 1991. 'The Pratītyasamutpādagāthā and its role in the medieval cult of the relics' in *Journal of the International Association of Buddhist Studies* 1991, 14: 1–27.

Broughton, Jeffrey L. *Zongmi on Chan*. New York: Columbia University Press, 2009.

Buswell, Jr. Robert E. *The Formation of Ch'an Ideology in China and Korea: The Vajrasamādhi-Sūtra, a Buddhist Apocryphon*. Princeton, NJ: Princeton University Press, 1989.

— *Cultivating Original Enlightenment: Wonhyo's Exposition of the Vajrasamādhi Sūtra*.Hawai'i: University of Hawai`i Press, 2008.

Campany, Robert Ford. *Signs from the Unseen Real. Buddhist Miracle Tales From Early China*. Kuroda Institute. Honolulu: University of Hawai'i Press, 2012.

Corbin, Henry. *Creative Imagination in the Ṣūfism of Ibn 'Arabi*. Oxon: Routledge, 2008. (Princeton: Princeton University Press, 1969).

Conze, Edward. *The Large Sutra of Perfect Wisdom*. Berkeley: University of California Press, 1975.

Harrison, Paul. *The Samādhi of Direct Encounter with the Buddhas of the Present: An Annotated English Translation of the Tibetan Version of the Pratyutpanna-Buddha-Saṃmukhāvasthita-Samādhi-Sūtra with Several Appendices Relating to the History of the Text (PraS)*. Tokyo: The International Institute for Buddhist Studies. Studia philologica

Buddhica, Monographs series 5, 1990.

Hummel, Arthur W. *Eminent Chinese of the Ch'ing Period 1644–1912*. 2 vols. Washington: Government Printing Office, 1943; Rprt: Folkestone, Kent: Global Oriental (Brill imprint), 2010.

Jones, Charles B. *Chinese Pure Land Buddhism, Understanding a Tradition of Practice*. Honolulu: University of Hawai'I Press, 2019.

Karashima, Seishi. 'Who were the icchantikas?'*Annual Report of the International Research Institute for Advanced Buddhology*: 67–80, 2007.

Keenan, John P. *The Scripture on Explanation of the Underlying Meaning*. Berkeley: Numata Center for Translation and Research, 2000.

Lamotte, Etienne. *Le traité de la grande vertu de sagesse*, Tome III. Louvain: Université de Louvain, 1970.

Lancaster, Lewis R. *An Analysis of the Aṣṭasāhasrikā-prajñāpāramitā-Sūtra from the Chinese Translations*. PhD. Diss., University of Wisconsin 1968; 1979.

Lusthaus, Dan. *Buddhist Phenomenology*. London: Routledge Curzon, 2002.

McRae, John R. *Seeing through Zen Encounter, Transformation, and Genealogy in Chinese Chan Buddhism*. Berkeley: University of California Press, 2003.

Muller, Charles. 'East Asian Apocryphal Scriptures: Their Origin and Role in the Development of Sinitic Buddhism,' in *Bulletin of Toyo Gakuen University*, vol. 6 (1998).

— 'Woncheuk 圓測 on Bimba 本質 and Pratibimba 影像 in his Commentary on the Saṃdhinirmocana-*Sūtra*' in *Journal of Indian and Buddhist Studies* Vol. 59, No.3, March 2011.

Ning Yu. *The Chinese consciousness in a Cognitive Perspective. Culture, Body, and Language.* Berlin: Mouton de Gruyter, 2009.

Nyanatiloka. *Visuddhi-Magga oder Der Weg Zur Reinheit.* Konstanz: Verlag Christiani, 1993.

Pitman, Don A. *Towards a Modern Chinese Buddhism. Taixu's Reforms.* Honolulu: Hawai'i University Press, 2001.

Radich, Michael. "Ideas about 'Consciousness' in Fifth and Sixth Century Chinese Buddhist Debates on the Survival of Death by the Spirit, and the Chinese Background to *Amalavijñāna," in Lin, Chen-kuo, (Ed.). *A Distant Mirror: Articulating Indic Ideas in Sixth and Seventh Century Chinese Buddhism.* Hamburg: Hamburg University Press, 2014.

Robson, James. *The Power of Place. The Religious Landscape of the Southern Sacred Peak* (*Nanyue* 南嶽) in Medieval China. Cambridge (Massachusetts): Harvard University Asia Center, 2009.

Rouzer, Paul. (trans.). *The Poetry of Hanshan (Cold Mountain), Shide, and Fenggan* Christopher M. B. Nugent (Ed.). Boston / Berlin: Walter de Gruyter, 2017.

Schuessler, Axel. *ABC Etymological Dictionary of Old Chinese.* Honolulu: Hawai'I University Press, 2007.

Slingerland, Edward. *Effortless Action Wu-wei as Conceptual Metaphor and Spiritual Ideal in Early China.* Oxford: Oxford University Press, 2003.

Swanson, Paul L. (trans.). *Clear Serenity, Quiet Insight* T'ien-t'ai Chih-I's *Mo-ho Chih-kuan,* 3 vols. Honolulu: University of Hawai'I Press, 2018.

Teng Weijen, 'On Kuiji's Sanskrit Compound Analyses' in Tansen Sen (Ed.). *Buddhism Across Asia Networks of Material, Intellectual and Cultural Exchange.* Singapore: Institute of Southeast Asian Studies, Manohar, 2014.

Thomas, Dylan. *Collected Poems 1934–1952.* London: Everyman's Library, 1966.

Wayman, Alex and Hideko Wayman, (trans.). *The Lion's Roar of Queen Śrīmālā.* New York: Columbia University Press, 1974.

Welter, Albert, F. *Yongming Yanshou's Conception of Chan in the Zongjing Lu. A Special Transmission within the Scriptures.* Oxford: Oxford University Press, 2011.

— *Monks, Rulers and Literati: The Political Ascendancy of Chan Buddhism.* Oxford: Oxford University Press, 2006.

— *The Linji Lu and the Creation of Chan Orthodoxy.* Oxford: Oxford University Press, 2008.

— *The Meaning of Myriad Good Deeds: A Study of Yung-ming Yen-shou and the Wan-shan t'ung-kuei chi (Treatise on the Common End of Myriad Good Deeds).* PhD. diss., Hamilton, Ontario: McMaster University, 1986.

Whitfield, Randolph S, (trans.). *Records of the Transmission of the Lamp.* 8 vols. Norderstedt: BoD, 2015–2020.

Wu, Jiang. *Enlightenment in Dispute. The Reinvention of Chan Buddhism in Seventeenth Century China.* Oxford: Oxford University Press, 2008.

Zacchetti, Stefano. *The Da zhidu lun* 大智度論 *(*Mahāprajñāpāramitopadeśa) and the

166

History of the Larger Prajñāpāramitā Patterns of Textual Variation in Mahāyāna Sūtra Literature. Michael Radich and Jonathan Silk (Eds.). Bochum / Greiburg: Project Verlag, Numata Center for Buddhist Studies, Hamburg Buddhist Series 14, 2021.

Zürcher, Eric. *The Buddhist Conquest of China.* 2 vols. Leiden: E. J. Brill, 1972.

—— "Perspectives in the Study of Chinese Buddhism," *Journal of the Royal Asiatic Society* 1982 (2): 161–176.

—— *Het leven van de Boeddha : Xiuconsciousnessg Benqi jing & Zhong benqi jing.* (Translated into Dutch). Amsterdam: Meulenhoff, 1978.

Index I

Questions addressed by Yongming Yanshou
Fascicle Two

421b19

Now, the realm of all the Buddhas is quiescent, the world of living beings emp-ty. What then are the causes and conditions giving rise to the marks of the Buddhas' teachings?

421c12

Question: Since there is a worry about grasping at the finger pointing [at the moon] and running after texts then, again, why be concerned about collecting teachings?

421c19

Question: All the major sutras and commentaries have come from so many fragments, with an ordering principle into divisions and prefaces. The mean-ings of the sentences are clarified, but why bring together the records of a big text artificially and complete it with a summary?

422a22

Question: To awaken to the meaning of the great vehicle of the Mahayana, expanded, abbreviated or all-inclusive, understanding one meaning confers the insight of perfect penetration; hearing one gatha has the merit of becoming a Buddha. Why presume to be able to relate it completely or bother with an elucidation?

423b18

Question: In general, to present and elucidate the great teaching in order to transform beings, it is necessary that one's own practice be completely accom-plished by having passed through the stages of personal realisation; only then will the original vow have been fulfilled. Then to open the gate of expedient means is of benefit, not counterfeit, neither will it be at odds with the correct teachings. That which is recorded here, has it been clearly realised?

424c05

Question: The gate to the teachings of expedient means of all the Buddhas relies on promoting (起) the root capacities of living beings. But root natures vary; dharmas are only dust and sand. The thirty-seven factors of enlightenment aid the entry to the Way, the fifty- two stages are the path of cultivating practice. So why posit only one consciousness as being the Ancestral Mirror [teachings]?

425a12

'Question: (Continuing the quote from T1667) "Above it is said that *thusness* is far from all characteristics, so how can it be said to be fully endowed with the characteristics of merit-producing power?"'

426b07

Question: The three realms are only consciousness, the myriad dharmas 'Only Consciousness'; should there be a teaching (宗) on thusness separate from these all-embracing dharmas?

426b17

Another question: The three realms contain contaminated outflows of dharmas, due to people being fettered by the bonds of desire in the three realms, hence the name three realms. But their unconditioned and uncontaminated dharmas are not tethered by desires for the three realms; that is, it is not called the Dharma of the three realms. Why then do sutras solely declare that the three realms are only consciousness, which really does not include (unite with 不攝) such as the unconditioned and uncontaminated dharmas? This is surely not [the doctrine of] 'Only Consciousness', for it only talks of three realms?

426b26

Question: How many entrances to meritorious power can evoke faith in what is seen and heard by establishing consciousness as the teaching?

427a02

Question: How could the one consciousness be regarded as the essential doc-

169

trine within the teachings? There is broad discussion of various ways and each is set up as a doctrinal theme of a sutra.

Questions addressed by Yongming Yanshou
Fascicle Three

0428a19

Now the teachings clarify the myriad dharmas – the ultimate principle is empty and profound. No explanations of existence or non-existence can cut through the nature of self and other, but if there is no intrinsic essence to any dharmas, how can one establish a teaching?

428b03

Question: By taking consciousness as the teaching, how is the characteristic of the teaching completely understood?

428b16

Question: Awakening to the path clarifies the teaching, like a person drinking water knows whether it is hot or cold, but say, how does this explain its defining activity?

430a24

Question: To take consciousness as the source teaching, principle is necessarily the definitive, yet in accord with the world of sentient beings. Truth and falsehood are seemingly divided and cannot be identified with one another. There is an excess of [opinions on] perfect enlightenment. It is like gold and copper being smelted together – the real and the counterfeit are suddenly separated, sand and rice cooked together come to a different fruition. Not yet understood – with which is consciousness taken as the teaching?

431b10

Question: The two 'consciousnesses' the deluded and the true – what is the meaning of calling each one 'consciousness'? What is 'essence'? What is 'characteristic'?

Question: What is the textual precedent for the defining activity of an awakened consciousness (真心)?

Question: Consciousness is able to become Buddha, consciousness produces a sentient being and with insight into the awakened consciousness (真心) one therefore becomes a Buddha. As a result of grasping onto the deluded consciousness one then becomes a sentient being. When one becomes a Buddha there is a full endowment of the five eyes of perfect penetration, without the defiled outflows of the five skandhas, therefore a sutra says, 'Eliminate the impermanent desires and acquire the permanent form,' and another says, 'The ineffable form is a deeply imbued and permanently abiding peace,' and yet again, 'The skilled are able to distinguish all dharma phenomena,' so why say that the awakened consciousness that does not abide in seeing, hearing, feeling and knowing is forever free from conceptual thinking?

Question: Where is the textual precedent for the defining activity of deluded mentation (妄心)?

Questions addressed by Yongming Yanshou
Fascicle Four

Now, there are those who speak of the dharma of consciousness, but say, what is consciousness, what is consciousness's dharma?

Question: This dharma of the one consciousness, how many interpretations (義) does it generate?

Question: Within the four interpretations of consciousness, the first two interpretations are conditioned by consciousness thinking delusively, whilst the last two concern the ever-abiding true consciousness. In short, the true consciousness is then the original nature's ineffable investigations of the principle of emptiness (空寂). Given the absence of an enumeration, there are no further indications, as it only involves the seemingly deluded consciousness's seeing and hearing. It is also said that birth and death is conditioned by the cognising consciousness – so how numerous are these defining activities (行相)?

434a22

An ancient worthy asked, 'The five states of consciousness within the eight consciousnesses – how many states of consciousness are there in each?'

434a26

Question: The seventh [consciousness] manifests discursive conceptualisations (計度分別), so why is there no searching consciousness present?

434a28

Question: Since the first five [consciousnesses] have an 'instantly-alighting' (率爾) [perception of an unidentified object], why is there no searching/investigation [state]?

434b03

Question: The eighth and the seventh [consciousnesses] constantly respond in concert to the present situation (object), so how could such [a state as an] 'instantly-alighting' [perception on an unidentified object] come about?

434b06

Question: Initially, at the time of undergoing birth, the seventh consciousness also initiates the three realms, but why is there no 'instantly alighting' consciousness in the eighth consciousness?

434b10

Question: Within the five states of consciousness, which [state] perfumes (impregnates, suffuses) the seeds and which do not perfume the seeds?

434c03

Question: By following a biased subjectivity (分別), a true and a deluded consciousness are set up; in general, how many kinds of these consciousnesses are there?

Question: Consciousness is designated by four names, revealing ten interpretations; exactly how many meanings are there to these names of consciousness?

Question: These statements only make the distinction (遮) that external objects do not exist; [but] there are distinctions between objects being separate from consciousness, from objects not separate from consciousness.

Question: [Given that] internal objects are part of consciousness, and since, moreover, it is not [that they are] non-existent, why then say that it is 'Only Consciousness', [why] not say 'only conscious objects'?

Question: The 'nature of Only Consciousness' and 'Only Consciousness' – are these the same or different?

Question: Approximately how many kinds of these 'Only Consciousnesses' are there?

General Index

'only consciousness', distinctions in, are ten, 143

'Only' and 'Consciousness' initially separating the explanations, 136

'only', three interpretations, 136

acknowledging the fire, it melts away of itself, but does not eliminate the person, 64

amalavijñāna, pure consciousness, 135

Ananda, 91, 95, 100

Aśvajit, 44

Bodhidharma, 75, 90, 95

branches, 89, 93, 105, 120-2, 125, 144

Chan School (禪宗), 87, 88

clever child, activity of, 105

Compound terms (持業釋) six kinds, 138, 140

Daoxuan, 65

death merely of discriminating consciousness, 118

deluded mind is the shadowy form of the true mind above it, 11, 92

deluded consciousness, 11, 88, 90, 92, 98, 99, 103, 109, 110, 118, 171

Dragon King, 71

eight consciousnesses, how many states of consciousness in each? 114, 172

eight errors, 109

eight sufferings, 109

enclosing walls, 88

errant thief, 87

esoteric teachings, 70

every situation an entry into dharma realm, 134

Everybody can be humanised just through faith, 39

explicit teachings, 70

faith, 24, 27, 30, 33, 35, 39, 46, 48, 63, 66, 107, 133, 151

Fazang, master, 25

five desires, 109

five interpretations of *xin's* distinguishing of characteristics, 63

five states or conditions of consciousness, 112, 114, 116

four correct opportunities, 87

four interpretations of consciousness, 112, 118

four Maras, 109

four raging streams, 109

four sacred Dharma realms, 128

Fu Dashi, 84

good Dharma-friend, 45

hairs of a tortoise, 92

Hanshan, verse of, 58

Heze, 70

horns of a rabbit, 83, 92

Huizhong, Imperial Preceptor, 47

'I', discussion of, 78

Indra's net, 126-7

instant-alighting perception, 114-15

internal realisation of own consciousness the first principle, 74

intrinsic nature (自體), 50, 63, 73, 89, 92, 94, 110, 136-7

Jiangxi (Mazu), 70

Layman Pang, 84

Mahāmati, 74

maintain the middle way (契會), 33

Mañjuśri, 59, 79, 82, 149

Mara, 46, 88

monkeys, 104

nine conditions for arising, 99

nine interpretations of the noumenal and phenomenal (性相), 135

174

one thought-moment, 13 (n. 19), 87, 127, 147

Only Consciousness not excluded from expansion or contraction, 136

ordinary consciousness is the Buddha-consciousness, 110

recorded here, been clearly realised?, 39

Rong, Great master Farong, 149

Śāriputra, 44

Second Patriarch [of Chan, Huike], 90, 95

seed passing through the aeons, 36

Sima Biao, 61

single phrase attained, spirit is entered, 35

six worldly realms of dharma, 128

Subhūti, 80, 131

Sudhana, 59

tathāgatagharba in bondage to the Dharma-body, 119, 120

ten defilements, 109

ten kinds of moral behaviours, 107, 109

ten realms of dharma, 128

three consciousnesses active in the external world, 89

three contemplations, the, 56, 70

true consciousness, 59, 87, 89, 95, 151

true, false, defiled or pure, the non-dual nature of all dharmas, 54

two emptinesses, pernicious attachment to, 24

two kinds of roots, birth/death and beginningless bodhi, 88

two penetrations, 76

verbal construct, all is, 40

whirlpools, 127

Yellow Court Classic, 118